AF605035

SLOW
COOKED
Comfort Food
New
Idea

SLOW
COOKED
Comfort Food

Contents

Simple SLOW COOKER

Making delicious meals couldn't be any easier with a slow cooker as your kitchen helper.

SERVES 6

TIP
This spice rub is perfect added to a curry; rub over beef and lamb steaks or chicken fillets or toss through vegetables before roasting. Place any leftover curry in a freezer-proof container and freeze for up to two months.

South African Beef Curry

PREP & COOK 5 HOURS, 50 MINS

- 2 brown onions, finely chopped
- 4 cloves garlic, crushed
- ¼ cup South African spice mix (see recipe below)
- 2kg beef chuck steak, trimmed, cut into 4cm pieces
- 400g can diced tomatoes
- 2 beef stock cubes, crumbled
- 1 tblsp cornflour
- Brown rice and quinoa and chopped fresh parsley, to serve

SOUTH AFRICAN SPICE MIX

- 2 tblsps ground coriander
- 1 tblsp ground cumin
- 1 tblsp turmeric
- 2 tsps ground cardamon
- 1 tsp cayenne pepper
- 1 tsp allspice
- 1 tsp cinnamon

1 Heat an oiled, large frying pan over a medium to high heat. Add onions and garlic. Cook stirring for about 3 minutes, or until soft. Stir in spice mix. Cook, stirring for 1 minute, or until fragrant.

2 Combine onions with beef, tomatoes and stock cubes in the removable bowl of a 5- to 6-litre capacity slow cooker. Season with salt and pepper. Toss to combine. Cover with lid.

3 Cook on LOW for 5 to 5 hours and 30 minutes, or until beef is tender.

4 Blend cornflour with 2 tblsps water in a small jug. Add to slow cooker. Stir until combined. Cook a further 10 minutes, or until slightly thickened.

5 Serve with rice and quinoa. Scatter over chopped parsley.

SOUTH AFRICAN SPICE MIX Place all ingredients in a small bowl. Mix well. Transfer to an airtight jar. Store in a cool, dry place for up to two months. (Makes ½ cup)

SERVES 6-8

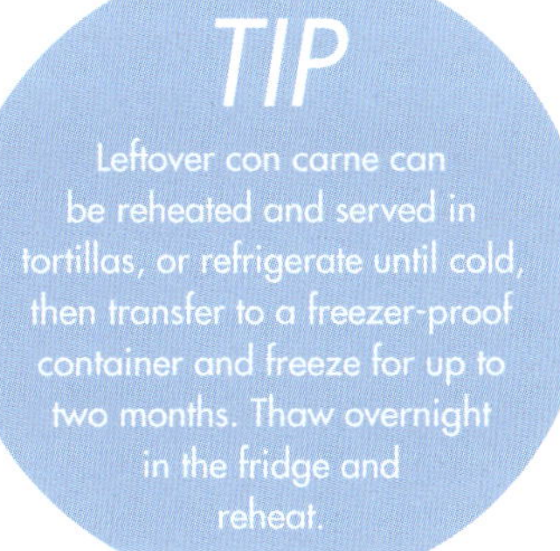

Beef Chilli Con Carne

PREP & COOK 7 HOURS, 30 MINS

2kg beef chuck steak, trimmed, cut into 3cm pieces
2 large onions, coarsely chopped
35g sachet chilli seasoning
3 tsps ground coriander
⅓ cup tomato paste
2 x 400g cans red kidney beans, drained, rinsed
400g can crushed tomatoes
1 cup fresh coriander leaves, plus extra to garnish
Steamed rice, sour cream, smashed avocado and tortilla strips, to serve

1 Place beef, onions, seasoning, ground coriander, paste, kidney beans and tomatoes in a removable bowl of a 5- to 6-litre slow cooker. Stir to combine. Cover with lid.

2 Cook on LOW for about 7 hours, or until beef is tender. Stir in coriander.

3 Serve with rice, sour cream, smashed avocado and tortilla strips. Garnish with extra coriander.

This dish is best cooked on a low setting. Beef blade roast is available from the butcher section of major supermarkets. Any flavoured liquid gravy can be used in this recipe.

SERVES 8

Beef in Mustard Pepper Gravy with Potatoes and Carrots

PREP & COOK 7 HOURS, 55 MINS

4 large carrots, trimmed, peeled
500g baby red potatoes
8 pickling onions, peeled, halved
4 cloves garlic, peeled
2 sprigs fresh rosemary
2 x 1kg beef blade roast
2 x 160g sachets Pepper and Shiraz liquid gravy
¼ cup wholegrain mustard
2 beef stock cubes, crumbled
2 tblsps cornflour
Steamed green beans, to serve

1 Cut carrots in half lengthways, then in half crossways.

2 Combine carrots, potatoes, onions, garlic and rosemary in the removable bowl of a 5- to 6-litre capacity slow cooker. Top with beef.

3 Combine gravy and mustard in a jug. Whisk well. Pour over beef. Add stock cubes. Cover with lid.

4 Cook on LOW for about 7 to 7 hours and 30 minutes, or until beef is tender. Remove beef and vegetables from bowl. Cover to keep warm.

5 Pour cooking liquid into a large saucepan over a high heat. Stir in cornflour blended with 2 tblsps water. Bring to boil, stirring for about 1 to 2 minutes, or until thickened. Pour gravy into a serving jug.

6 Serve beef with carrots, potatoes, onions and steamed beans. Drizzle with gravy.

SERVES 6

Beef Massaman Curry

PREP & COOK 3 HOURS, 45 MINS

- 1.5kg beef gravy steak, trimmed, cut into 5cm pieces
- 800g chat potatoes
- 1 cinnamon stick
- 2 large onions, chopped
- 2 tblsps fresh ginger paste
- ½ cup massaman curry paste
- ½ cup beef stock
- 400ml can coconut milk
- 2 tblsps brown sugar
- 2 tblsps fish sauce
- ⅓ cup roasted unsalted peanuts, plus extra to serve
- Steamed rice and fresh coriander, to serve

1 Heat an oiled, large, non-stick frying pan over a high heat. Add beef in two batches. Cook, turning occasionally, until browned all over. Transfer to a removable bowl of a 5- to 6-litre capacity slow cooker. Add potatoes and cinnamon.

2 Reduce heat to medium. Add onion and ginger to same frying pan. Cook, stirring occasionally, until soft. Add curry paste. Cook, stirring, for 1 minute, or until fragrant. Add stock, milk, sugar, sauce and peanuts. Bring to boil. Transfer to slow cooker. Cover with lid.

3 Cook on HIGH for 3 hours 30 minutes, or until beef and potatoes are tender.

4 Serve with steamed rice. Garnish with peanuts and coriander.

SERVES 6-8

TIP

Tikka masala paste is mild in heat, you can use Rogan Josh or tandoori pastes instead. To cook pappadams in microwave, place around the outside of turntable plate and microwave on High (100%) for about 1 minute.

Chicken Tikka Masala Curry

PREP & COOK 5 HOURS, 45 MINS

2kg chicken thigh fillets, trimmed
800g Sebago potatoes, scrubbed, cut into 4cm pieces
1 large red onion, chopped
283g jar Tikka Masala paste
⅓ cup tomato paste
270g can coconut milk
2 chicken stock cubes, crumbled
Pappadams (see Tip), Greek yoghurt, mango chutney and fresh mint leaves, to serve

1 Place chicken, potatoes, onion, masala paste, tomato paste, milk and stock cubes in a removable bowl of a 5- to 6-litre capacity slow cooker. Stir to combine. Cover with lid.

2 Cook on LOW for about 5 to 5 hours and 30 minutes, or until chicken is cooked and potatoes are tender.

3 Serve with pappadams, combined yoghurt and chutney. Garnish with mint.

SERVES 6

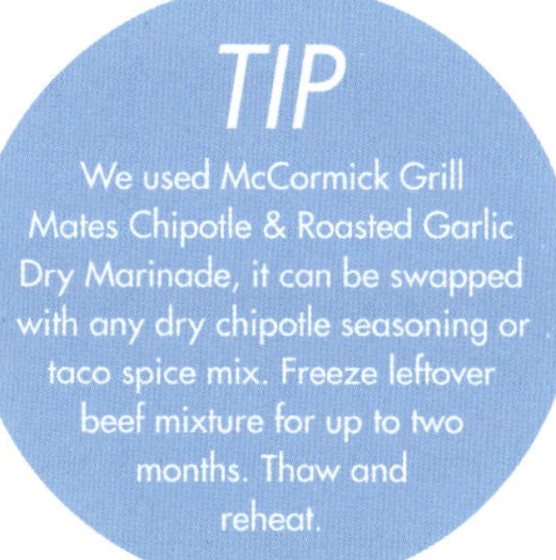

Cheesy Chipotle Beef Tacos

PREP & COOK 4 HOURS, 25 MINS

1.4kg beef chuck steak, trimmed
40g sachet Chipotle & Roasted Garlic Dry Marinade (see Tip)
400g can diced tomatoes
2 cups grated Tasty cheese
156g packet (12) taco shells
1 large avocado, mashed
Fresh coriander leaves, to serve

1 Toss beef with marinade in a large bowl.

2 Heat an oiled, large, non-stick frying pan over a high heat. Add beef in two batches. Cook for about 3 minutes on each side, or until browned. Transfer to a removeable bowl of a 5- to 6- litre capacity slow cooker. Stir in tomatoes. Cover with lid.

3 Cook on LOW for 4 hours, or until beef is tender. Using tongs, remove beef from cooker. Shred into thin strands. Return to cooker. Stir to coat.

4 Sprinkle 2 tblsps cheese on the inside of each taco shell. Place on a large oven tray lined with baking paper.

5 Cook in a moderately hot oven (200C) for about 5 minutes, or until cheese is melted and tacos are light golden.

6 Serve taco shells with avocado, beef, chopped tomato and coriander leaves.

SERVES 8

Curry can be made up to two days ahead. Keep, covered, in the fridge, or divide into individual portions in freezer-proof containers. Seal, date, label and freeze for up to two months.

Butter Chicken

PREP & COOK 5 HOURS, 40 MINS

2.5kg chicken thigh fillets, trimmed
1 large onion, halved, thinly sliced
1 tblsp fresh ginger paste
1 tsp garam masala
2 x 375g sachets Butter Chicken Simmer Sauce
300ml tub light thickened cooking cream
2 tblsps tomato paste
Fresh coriander leaves, to garnish
Steamed basmati rice and warm naan bread, to serve

1 Combine chicken, onion, ginger and garam masala in the removable bowl of a 5- to 6-litre capacity slow cooker. Toss well to coat. Add simmer sauce, cream and tomato paste. Stir to combine. Cover with lid.

2 Cook on LOW for about 5 hours and 30 minutes, or until chicken is cooked and sauce is thickened.

3 Garnish curry with coriander. Serve with rice and naan bread.

SERVES 6

TIP

Store any leftover soup, chicken and noodles separately, in the fridge for up to three days; reheat until hot just before serving. Soup and chicken can be frozen in individual freezer-proof containers up to one month. Thaw overnight in the fridge.

Chicken Pho

PREP & COOK 4 HOURS, 30 MINS

1 litre (4 cups) chicken stock
1 large onion, halved, thinly sliced
8cm piece ginger (80g), peeled, thinly sliced
2 tblsps coriander seeds
2 tsps whole black peppercorns
4 whole cloves
4 star anise
⅓ cup fish sauce
1 tblsp brown sugar
1.2kg chicken thigh fillets, trimmed
375g packet dried rice noodles
Bean sprouts, Vietnamese mint leaves, sliced red chilli and lime wedges, to serve

1 Combine stock, onion, ginger, spices, fish sauce, sugar and 2 litres (8 cups) of water in the removable bowl of a 5- to 6-litre capacity slow cooker. Add chicken. Cover with lid.

2 Cook on LOW for 4 hours, or until chicken is cooked through. Using a slotted spoon, remove chicken from soup. Cool slightly. Thinly shred.

3 Meanwhile, cook noodles according to packet directions until tender. Drain.

4 Place a sieve over a large bowl. Strain hot soup in batches through sieve. Discard onion and spices. Return soup to slow cooker and keep warm on LOW.

5 To serve, divide noodles and shredded chicken among serving bowls. Ladle over soup. Top with sprouts, mint and chilli. Serve with lime wedges.

SERVES 8-10

Chipotle and Bean Nachos Mince

PREP & COOK 6 HOURS, 15 MINS

2 red onions, finely chopped
1 tblsp fresh garlic paste
1 red capsicum, chopped
1 green capsicum, chopped
1.5kg beef mince
2 x 35g sachets chipotle seasoning
410g can tomato puree
400g can kidney beans, drained, rinsed
375g jar chunky mild salsa
2 beef stock cubes, crumbled
Corn chips, chopped avocado, tomatoes, fresh coriander and sour cream, to serve

1 Place onions, garlic and capsicums in the removable bowl of a 5- to 6-litre capacity slow cooker. Stir to combine. Add mince. Stir to break up mince. Sprinkle over seasoning.

2 Add puree, beans, salsa and stock cubes. Stir to combine. Cover with lid.

3 Cook on LOW for about 6 hours, or until beef is cooked and sauce is thickened.

4 Serve with corn chips, avocado, sour cream, chopped tomatoes and coriander.

SERVES 6

To remove the fat off the sauce, use a large metal spoon and skim it across the surface. This dish can be cooked on HIGH in Step 4 for 5 hours, or until lamb is tender.

Greek Leg of Lamb

PREP & COOK 7 HOURS, 25 MINS

2kg leg of lamb, bone-in
4 cloves garlic, peeled, sliced
1kg chat potatoes
4 large carrots, cut into 6cm lengths
½ cup dry white wine
40g sachet Slow Cooker Greek Lamb Recipe Base
Lemon wedges, to serve
Fresh oregano leaves, to garnish

1 Using a sharp knife, cut 3cm deep slits, about 4cm apart, over top of lamb. Insert garlic into slits. Season with salt and pepper.

2 Heat a large, non-stick frying pan over a high heat. Add lamb. Cook, turning occasionally, for about 8 minutes, or until browned all over. Transfer to a removable bowl of a 5- to 6-litre capacity slow cooker with potatoes and carrots.

3 Whisk wine into recipe base in a small jug. Pour over lamb and vegetables. Cover with lid.

4 Cook on a LOW for about 7 hours, or until meat is tender and falling off the bone. Remove lamb and vegetables. Skim fat off the top of sauce in slow cooker.

5 Serve lamb and vegetables with lemon wedges and sauce. Garnish with oregano.

SERVES 6-8

TIP

A smoked ham hock is available from most major supermarkets. Soup can be divided into individual portions in freezer-proof containers. Seal, date and label. Freeze for up to two months.

Ham Hock Soup

PREP & COOK 11 HOURS, 25 MINS

- 2 onions, finely chopped
- 1 small fennel, finely chopped
- 1 large carrot, peeled, finely chopped
- 3 stalks celery, finely chopped
- 1 dried bay leaf
- ⅓ cup tomato paste
- 1 cup dried soup mix (200g)
- 1kg smoked ham hock
- 1 litre (4 cups) chicken stock
- 1.5 litres (6 cups) water
- 1 bunch English spinach, trimmed, washed, shredded
- Crusty bread, to serve

1 Place onions, fennel, carrot, celery and bay leaf in the removable bowl of a 5- to 6-litre capacity slow cooker. Stir in paste and soup mix. Top with ham. Pour over stock and water. Cover with lid.

2 Cook on LOW for 10 to 11 hours, or on HIGH for about 8 to 9 hours, or until ham is tender and falling away from the bone. Remove ham from soup. Cool slightly.

3 Shred ham, discarding skin and bones. Return ham meat to slow cooker with spinach. Stir to combine.

4 Serve with crusty bread.

Whole champignons are available in the canned vegetable section of most supermarkets. Cacciatore can be made up to three days ahead. Keep, covered, in the fridge.

SERVES 6

Meatball Cacciatore

PREP & COOK 4 HOURS, 30 MINS

1 onion, finely chopped
1 large red capsicum, cut into 2cm pieces
400g can whole champignons, drained
2 x 400g cans diced tomatoes
½ cup dry white wine
2 tblsps tomato paste
2 tblsps baby capers, drained
2 cloves garlic, crushed
1 beef stock cube, crumbled
½ cup pitted kalamata olives
Chopped fresh parsley, to garnish
Crusty bread and steamed green beans, to serve

MEATBALLS

80g tube fresh Italian Herbs paste
1kg pork and veal mince
⅓ cup dried packaged breadcrumbs
1 egg, lightly beaten

1 To make meatballs, set aside 2 tblsps of the Italian herbs paste in a small bowl. Squeeze remaining paste into a large bowl with mince, breadcrumbs and egg. Season with salt and pepper. Mix well. Roll two heaped tablespoons into balls. (Makes about 18.)

2 Place onion in the removable bowl of a 5- to 6-litre capacity slow cooker. Add capsicum, champignons, tomatoes, wine, tomato paste, capers, garlic and stock cube. Stir in reserved herbs paste. Season with salt and pepper. Stir well.

3 Arrange meatballs over the capsicum mixture, gently pressing into the sauce. Cover with lid.

4 Cook on LOW for about 4 hours, or until meatballs are cooked through. Stir in olives.

5 Garnish with chopped parsley. Serve with crusty bread and steamed green beans.

SERVES 6

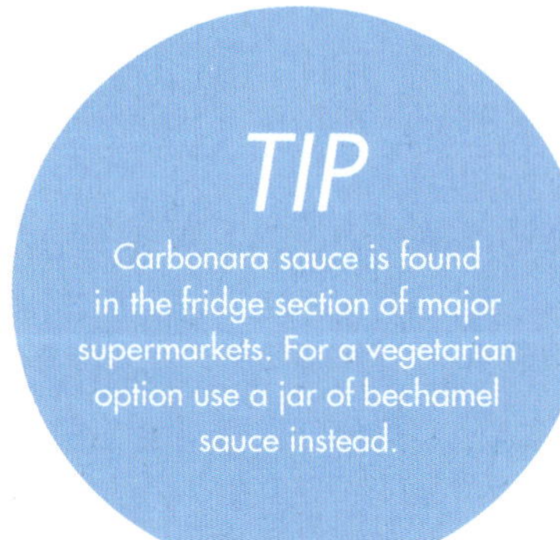

Lasagne Lovers

PREP & COOK 5 HOURS

2 large zucchini (500g), peeled into ribbons
425g tub fresh carbonara pasta sauce
1⅓ cups grated mozzarella
6 instant lasagne sheets
Garlic pizza bread, to serve

VEGIE SAUCE

350g jar Stir Through Sauce Roasted Vegetables
310g jar roasted capsicum strips, drained
120g tub chargrilled eggplant, drained, chopped
¼ cup chopped fresh basil, plus leaves to garnish

1 Lightly grease a removeable bowl of a 5- to 6-litre capacity slow cooker.

2 To make vegie sauce, combine all ingredients in a large jug.

3 To assemble, spread one-third of the vegie sauce over the base of slow cooker bowl. Top with one-third of the zucchini, followed by ⅓ cup carbonara sauce, ⅓ cup cheese and two lasagne sheets, broken to fit. Repeat layers twice. Top with remaining carbonara sauce and cheese.

4 Cook on LOW for about 4 hours and 30 minutes, or until lasagne is tender and cheese is lightly browned. Turn power off. Stand, covered, for 20 minutes. Remove bowl from slow cooker.

5 Serve with pizza bread. Garnish with basil leaves.

SERVES 4

TIP

Try replacing dried cranberries, with apricots or prunes instead. This recipe can be cooked on LOW for about 7 to 8 hours, or until lamb is tender.

Lamb Tagine

PREP & COOK 4 HOURS, 20 MINS

900g lamb shoulder, cut into 4cm pieces
1 onion, chopped
3 carrots, cut into 3cm pieces
1 tblsp tomato paste
2 tsps ras-el-hanout
1 tsp ground cumin
1 beef stock cube, crumbled
1 large sweet potato, cut into 4cm pieces
30g dried cranberries
1 tsp honey
Cooked couscous and chopped fresh coriander, to serve

1 Heat an oiled, large non-stick frying pan over a high heat. Add lamb in two batches. Cook, turning until browned. Transfer to the removable bowl of a 5- to 6-litre capacity slow cooker.

2 Add onion to same pan. Cook, stirring for 5 minutes, or until soft. Stir in carrots, tomato paste, spices, stock cube and 3 cups water. Bring to boil. Pour into slow cooker. Stir in sweet potato, cranberries and honey. Cover with lid.

3 Cook on HIGH for 4 hours, or until lamb is tender.

4 Serve with couscous. Garnish with chopped coriander.

SERVES 8

Mediterranean Lamb Shoulder

PREP & COOK 7 HOURS, 15 MINS

2 x 1kg rolled boneless lamb shoulders
1kg sweet potato, peeled, cut into 5cm pieces
2 red onions, finely chopped
80g tube fresh Mediterranean seasoning paste
1 tblsp finely grated lemon rind
¼ cup lemon juice
2 tblsps fresh thyme leaves
1 tblsp olive oil
2 chicken stock cubes, crumbled
Lemon wedges, to serve

OLIVE GREMOLATA

½ cup chopped pitted Sicilian olives
½ cup finely chopped fresh parsley
1 tblsp finely grated lemon rind

1 Remove and discard string from lamb.

2 Place sweet potato and onions in the removable bowl of a 5- to 6-litre capacity slow cooker. Place lamb shoulders, side by side, on top.

3 Combine paste, rind, juice, thyme and oil in a small bowl. Mix well. Spoon over lamb. Season with salt and pepper. Dissolve stock cubes in ½ cup boiling water. Pour over lamb. Cover with lid.

4 Cook on LOW for about 7 hours, or until lamb and potatoes are tender. Remove lamb from slow cooker. Thickly shred. Cover with foil to keep warm.

5 Using a slotted spoon, transfer sweet potato pieces to a serving plate. Cover to keep warm.

6 Skim excess fat from top of liquid in bowl. Transfer liquid to a large saucepan. Bring to boil. Boil for about 12 minutes, or until reduced by half. Pour into a heatproof jug.

7 Meanwhile, to make olive gremolata, combine all ingredients in a bowl. Season.

8 Serve sweet potato topped with lamb. Pour over sauce. Sprinkle with gremolata. Serve with lemon wedges.

SERVES 6-8

Smokin Texas Pork Ribs

PREP & COOK 4 HOURS, 15 MINS

40g sachet Smokin Texas BBQ Rub (see Tip)
⅔ cup barbecue sauce
1 tblsp Worcestershire sauce
1 tblsp brown sugar
1.8kg pork ribs, cut into 6cm lengths
450g bag Slaw Kit
Cooked fries, to serve

1 Combine rub, sauces and sugar in a medium jug.

2 Pour ½ cup sauce into a removeable bowl of a 5- to 6-litre slow cooker. Add 1½ cups water. Stir to combine. Transfer remaining sauce into a small saucepan. Set aside.

3 Add ribs to slow cooker, turn to coat in sauce. Cover with lid.

4 Cook on HIGH for 4 hours, or until ribs are tender. Transfer ribs to a large bowl. Cover with foil to keep warm. Reserve 1½ cups cooking liquid.

5 Add reserved cooking liquid to saucepan. Stir to combine. Gently boil for about 5 minutes, or until slightly thickened.

6 Combine ingredients from slaw kit in a bowl.

7 Pour three-quarters of the sauce over ribs. Toss to combine.

8 Serve ribs, drizzled with remaining sauce, coleslaw and fries.

SERVES 8

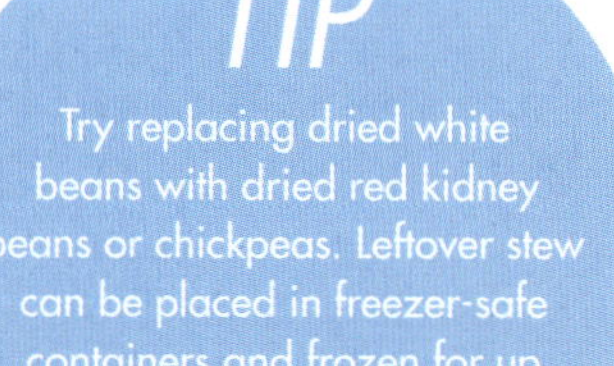

Spicy Vegetable and Bean Stew

PREP & COOK 10 HOURS, 15 MINS

2 cups dried white beans
2 tblsps olive oil
2 onions, finely chopped
2 red capsicums, chopped
3 cloves garlic, crushed
1 tblsp smoked paprika
1 tblsp ground cumin
2 tsps ground coriander
700g jar tomato passata cooking sauce
1 litre (4 cups) vegetable stock
2 tblsps hot chilli sauce
1kg sweet potato, peeled, cut into 2cm pieces
Chopped fresh parsley, to garnish
Crusty bread, to serve

1 Place beans in a bowl covered in cold water. Refrigerate, covered, overnight to soak. Drain. Rinse well. Place in the removable bowl of a 5- to 6-litre capacity slow cooker.

2 Heat oil in a large frying pan over a medium heat. Add onions, capsicums and garlic. Cook, stirring occasionally, until soft. Add spices. Cook, stirring, for 1 minute. Add to slow cooker with passata, stock and sauce. Season with salt and pepper. Cover with lid.

3 Cook on LOW for 7 hours.

4 Add sweet potato. Cook, covered, for a further 2 to 3 hours, or until beans and sweet potato are tender.

5 Garnish stew with chopped parsley. Serve with crusty bread.

SERVES 6

Spinach and Mushroom Lasagne

PREP & COOK 4 HOURS, 25 MINS.

200g punnet sliced mushrooms
280g bag baby spinach leaves
750g fresh ricotta
1⅔ cups grated Perfect Bakes cheese
425g tub fresh Napoli pasta sauce
6 instant lasagne sheets
Fresh basil leaves and rocket leaves, to serve

1 Lightly grease a removeable bowl of a 5- to 6-litre capacity slow cooker.

2 Heat an oiled, large, non-stick frying pan over a high heat. Add mushrooms. Cook, stirring for 3 minutes, or until soft. Add spinach. Cook, stirring until just wilted. Drain. Transfer mixture to a bowl. Cool slightly. Add ricotta and ⅓ cup grated cheese. Season with salt and pepper. Mix well.

3 To assemble, spread ⅓ cup sauce over base of slow cooker bowl. Spoon over 1½ cups spinach mixture, followed by ⅓ cup grated cheese and two lasagne sheets, broken to fit. Repeat layers twice with sauce, spinach mixture, cheese and lasagne sheets. Top with remaining sauce and cheese. Cover with lid.

4 Cook on LOW for about 4 hours, or until lasagne is tender and cheese is lightly browned. Turn power off. Stand, covered, for 20 minutes. Remove bowl from slow cooker.

5 Serve with basil and rocket leaves.

SERVES 4-6

Tom Yum Chicken Noodle Soup

PREP & COOK 4 HOURS, 50 MINS

1.4kg whole chicken
8 green spring onions, trimmed
⅓ cup tom yum paste
100g punnet shitake mushrooms, sliced
2 bunches choy sum, trimmed, roughly chopped
200g packet dried rice stick noodles
Chilli oil and lime wedges, to serve

1 Pat chicken dry with absorbent kitchen paper. Transfer to a removeable bowl of a 5- to 6-litre capacity slow cooker.

2 Cut 6 onions into 3cm lengths. Add to slow cooker. Cut remaining onions diagonally into thin slices. Set aside.

3 Add paste and 2 litres (8 cups) water to slow cooker. Cover with lid. Cook on LOW for 4 hours and 30 minutes.

4 Remove chicken. Cool slightly. Remove and discard skin and bones from chicken. Break chicken into large pieces. Return to slow cooker.

5 Stir in mushrooms and choy sum. Cover with lid. Cook for a further 5 minutes, or until mushrooms are tender and greens are just wilted.

6 Meanwhile, cook noodles according to packet directions until tender. Drain.

7 To serve, divide noodles among bowls. Pour in soup. Serve with reserved onions, chilli oil and lime wedges.

SERVES 6-8

Devilled Lamb Chops

PREP & COOK 7 HOURS, 15 MINS

2 large onions, coarsely chopped
500g carrots, peeled, cut into 3cm pieces
500g brushed potatoes, thickly sliced (1cm)
2kg lamb chump chops, trimmed
¼ cup traditional gravy powder
2 tblsps plain flour
½ cup Worcestershire sauce
⅓ cup tomato paste
2 tblsps Dijon mustard
1 tblsp brown sugar
2 beef stock cubes, crumbled
Chopped fresh parsley, crusty bread and steamed green beans, to serve

1 Place onions, carrots and potatoes in a removable bowl of a 7-litre capacity slow cooker.

2 In a large snap-lock bag, combine lamb, gravy powder and flour. Shake until lamb is well coated. Place over vegetables in slow cooker.

3 In a large jug, combine sauce, paste, mustard, sugar, stock cubes with ¾ cup of water. Pour mixture over the lamb. Cover with cooker lid.

4 Cook on LOW for about 6 to 7 hours, or until lamb and vegetables are tender.

5 Garnish with parsley. Serve with crusty bread and beans.

SERVES 6

TIP

Browning the chicken first will give the dish more flavour. Steps 1 and 2 can be prepared the night before. Keep covered in the fridge. Next day, continue with steps 3 and 4, cooking for an extra 30 minutes.

Tuscan Chicken

PREP & COOK 4 HOURS, 30 MINS

- 2 tblsps plain flour
- 1 tblsp ground paprika
- 1 tblsp garlic powder
- 2kg chicken thigh fillets, trimmed
- 250g punnet cherry tomatoes
- 220g jar sun-dried tomato strips, drained
- 300ml tub cooking light thickened cream
- 1 chicken stock cube, crumbled
- 60g baby spinach leaves
- Cooked penne pasta, to serve

1 Combine flour, paprika and garlic powder in a large bowl. Season with salt and pepper. One at a time, dust chicken pieces in seasoned flour, shaking off excess.

2 Heat an oiled, large, non-stick frying pan over a high heat. Cook chicken in three batches, for about 3 minutes each side, or until browned, adding more oil with each batch. Transfer to the removable bowl of a 5- to 6-litre capacity slow cooker.

3 Stir in cherry tomatoes, tomato strips, cream and stock cube. Cover with lid.

4 Cook on LOW for about 4 hours, or until chicken is cooked. Stir in spinach.

5 Serve with pasta.

SERVES 6

Spicy Apricot Chicken

PREP & COOK 4 HOURS, 20 MINS

2 tblsps plain flour
2 tsps ground cumin
2 tsps ground coriander
12 (2kg) chicken drumsticks
2 onions, halved, thinly sliced
225g packet dried apricots
⅓ cup apricot jam
⅓ cup soy sauce
2 tblsps hot English mustard
Cooked couscous and fresh coriander leaves, to serve

1 Combine flour and spices in a large bowl. Season with salt and pepper. One at a time, dust chicken drumsticks in seasoned flour, shaking off excess.

2 Heat an oiled, large non-stick frying pan over a medium-high heat. Cook chicken in two batches, turning occasionally, until browned all over, adding more oil, if needed. Transfer to the removable bowl of a 5- to 6-litre capacity slow cooker. Add onions and apricots. Stir in combined jam, sauce, mustard and ½ cup water. Cover with lid.

3 Cook on LOW for about 4 hours, or until chicken is cooked.

4 Serve with couscous. Garnish with coriander leaves.

Delicious COMFORT FOODS

Packed full of flavour, these comforting family favourites make perfect weeknight dinners.

SERVES 4

Beef and Mushroom Casserole

PREP & COOK 2 HOURS, 35 MINS

2 tblsps olive oil
1.2kg chuck steak, trimmed, cut into 3cm pieces
1 large onion, finely chopped
4 carrots (400g), thickly sliced diagonally
2 large stalks celery, sliced
200g button mushrooms
2 tblsps tomato paste
40g sachet French onion soup mix
2 cups beef stock
250g loaf garlic bread, coarsely chopped
Olive oil cooking spray
½ cup grated mozzarella cheese
¼ cup coarsely chopped fresh parsley

1 Heat half the oil in a deep, flameproof casserole dish (14-cup capacity). Add beef in two batches. Cook, turning occasionally, for about 5 minutes, until browned. Remove.

2 Heat remaining oil in same dish. Add onion, carrots and celery. Cook stirring occasionally, for about 5 minutes, until lightly browned. Stir in mushrooms.

3 Return beef to dish. Season with pepper. Stir in tomato paste, soup mix and stock. Bring to boil. Cover with lid.

4 Cook in a slow oven (150C) for 2 hours, stirring halfway, or until beef is tender. Remove from oven. Increase oven temperature to hot (220C).

5 Uncover casserole. Scatter garlic bread over top. Spray with cooking oil. Sprinkle over cheese.

6 Cook uncovered in hot oven (220C) for about 10 minutes, or until bread is crisp and cheese is melted. Remove.

7 Serve sprinkled with parsley.

SERVES 6

Baked Moroccan Chicken and Pearl Couscous

PREP & COOK 1 HOUR

750g chicken thigh fillets, trimmed, halved
1½ tblsps Moroccan seasoning
1 large red onion, cut into thin wedges
3 carrots, peeled, coarsely chopped
2 tblsps tomato paste
1½ cups pearl couscous
500ml carton salt-reduced chicken stock
1 tblsp honey
½ cup pitted green olives
½ cup chopped fresh coriander, plus extra to serve
100g feta, crumbled
Lemon wedges, to serve

1 Place chicken in a large bowl. Sprinkle over seasoning. Toss to coat.

2 Heat an oiled, large, flameproof casserole dish (14-cup capacity) over medium to high heat. Add chicken. Cook for about 2 minutes on each side, or until browned. Remove. Add onion and carrot. Cook, stirring, until lightly browned. Add tomato paste. Cook, stirring, for a further 1 minute.

3 Stir in couscous, stock, honey and ⅓ cup water. Return chicken to dish. Stir to combine. Cover with lid or foil.

4 Cook in a moderate oven (180C) for about 35 minutes, or until liquid is absorbed and couscous is tender. Stir in olives and coriander. Scatter over feta. Stand covered for 5 minutes.

5 Sprinkle with extra coriander. Serve with lemon wedges.

SERVES 6-8

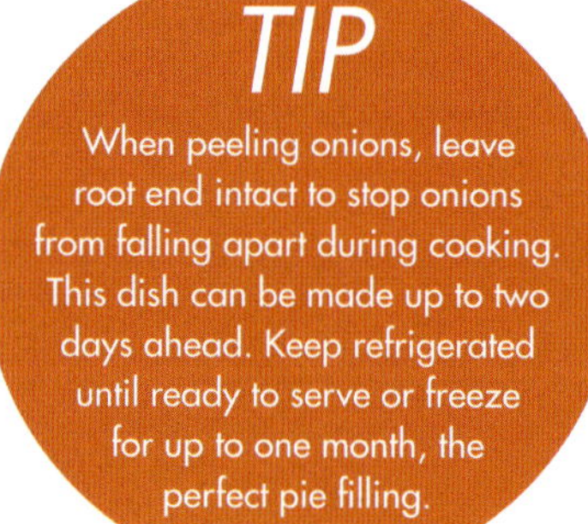

Beef Bourguignon

PREP & COOK 2 HOURS, 35 MINS

2kg gravy beef steak, trimmed, cut into 5cm pieces
⅓ cup plain flour
200g rashers streaky bacon, cut into 3cm pieces
200g button mushrooms
200g Swiss brown mushrooms
3 cloves garlic, crushed
12 pickling onions (500g), peeled
2 tblsps tomato paste
2 cups dry red wine
1 cup beef stock
3 sprigs fresh thyme, plus extra to garnish
2 bay leaves
Mashed potato and steamed green beans, to serve

1 Toss beef in flour seasoned with salt and pepper. Shake off excess.

2 Heat an oiled, large flameproof casserole dish (16-cup capacity) or stockpot over a high heat. Add beef in three batches. Cook, turning occasionally for about 4 minutes, or until browned all over. Remove.

3 Heat same oiled dish over a high heat. Add bacon, mushrooms and garlic. Cook, stirring for about 5 minutes, or until lightly browned. Stir in onions. Add paste. Stir for 30 seconds.

4 Return beef to dish with wine. Bring to boil. Stir in stock and herbs. Season with salt and pepper. Cover with lid.

5 Gently boil, stirring regularly during cooking, for about 2 hours, or until beef is tender.

6 Serve with mashed potato and beans. Garnish with extra thyme.

SERVES 4

Chicken and Vegetable Soup with Herb Pesto

PREP & COOK 50 MINS

2 stalks celery, chopped
1 large carrot, peeled, chopped
1 medium brown onion, chopped
2 cloves garlic, crushed
1 large potato, peeled, chopped
1.5 litres (6 cups) chicken stock
800g chicken thighs fillets, trimmed
Toasted bread, to serve

HERB PESTO

1 cup firmly packed fresh parsley leaves
⅓ cup olive oil
⅓ cup pine nuts, toasted
⅓ cup grated parmesan

1 Heat an oiled stockpot over a high heat. Add celery, carrot, onion and garlic. Cook, stirring occasionally for about 5 minutes, or until onion is soft.

2 Add potato. Cook for 2 minutes. Stir in stock and chicken. Season with salt and pepper. Bring to boil. Gently boil, covered for about 25 minutes, or until chicken is cooked.

3 Remove chicken from pot. Shred chicken into large pieces. Return shredded chicken to pot.

4 Meanwhile to make pesto, place all ingredients in a small food processor, blend until a smooth. Season with salt and pepper.

5 Serve soup with pesto and bread.

SERVES 4

Gnocchi Boscaiola Bake

PREP & COOK 40 MINS

500g packet fresh gnocchi
200g packet shortcut bacon rashers, chopped
200g cup mushrooms, sliced
300ml tub light thickened cooking cream
100g baby spinach leaves
1½ cups grated Perfect Melt 4 Cheeses

1 Cook gnocchi according to packet directions until tender. Drain.

2 Heat an oiled, large frying pan over high heat. Add bacon. Cook, stirring occasionally for about 4 minutes, or until golden. Add mushrooms. Cook, stirring for a further 3 minutes, or until soft.

3 Add cream and ¼ cup water. Bring to boil. Gently boil for 2 minutes. Remove from heat. Add gnocchi and spinach. Season with salt and pepper. Stir to combine. Transfer to an ovenproof dish (8-cup capacity). Sprinkle with cheese.

4 Cook in a moderately hot oven (200C) for about 15 minutes, or until cheese is melted and golden brown. Serve.

ECOLOGY™

SERVES 6

Harissa Lamb Hot Pot

PREP & COOK 1 HOUR, 25 MINS

1 tblsp olive oil
1kg diced lamb
1 large onion, thinly sliced
2 cloves garlic, crushed
2 tblsps harissa spice blend
140g tub (½ cup) tomato paste
500g small carrots, halved lengthways
2 cups chicken stock
420g can chickpeas, drained, rinsed
1 tblsp honey
½ cup coarsely chopped fresh coriander, plus leaves to garnish
Steamed green beans, cooked couscous and lemon wedges, to serve

1 Heat half the oil in a stockpot over a medium to high heat. Add lamb in two batches. Cook, turning occasionally, for about 5 minutes, until browned. Remove.

2 Heat remaining oil in pan. Add onion and garlic. Cook, stirring for about 3 minutes, until onion is soft. Add spice blend and tomato paste. Cook, stirring a further 1 minute. Return lamb to pot.

3 Stir in carrots, stock and 2 cups water. Bring to boil. Reduce heat. Simmer, covered for 1 hour.

4 Stir in chickpeas and honey. Simmer, uncovered for 15 to 20 minutes, or until lamb is tender and liquid is slightly thickened. Stir in coriander.

5 Serve with beans, couscous and lemon wedges. Garnish with coriander leaves.

SERVES 4-6

Chilli Con Carne Meatball Bake

PREP & COOK 55 MINS

750g pork and beef mince
1 small onion, finely chopped
41g sachet Chilli Con Carne Recipe Base
1 red capsicum, thinly sliced
400g can diced tomatoes with basil and oregano
420g can Chilli Beanz Medium
200g round corn chips
1 cup grated mozzarella
Chopped avocado, fresh coriander sprigs and sour cream, to serve

1 Combine mince, onion and recipe base in a large bowl. Season with salt and pepper. Roll mixture into 12 balls.

2 Heat a lightly oiled, large, deep flameproof dish (12-cup capacity) over a medium high heat. Add meatballs. Cook, turning for about 5 minutes, or until lightly browned all over. Remove meatballs from pan.

3 Add capsicum, tomatoes, Chilli Beanz and ⅓ cup water. Stir to combine. Return meatballs to pan. Stir until coated with sauce.

4 Cook in a moderately hot oven (200C) for about 20 minutes, or until meatballs are cooked and sauce has thickened slightly. Remove from oven. Increase oven to hot (220C).

5 Arrange corn chips over bake. Sprinkle with cheese. Return to oven.

6 Cook a further 10 minutes, or until lightly golden and cheese is melted.

7 Serve bake with avocado, coriander sprigs and sour cream.

SERVES 6

Cheesy Bubble and Squeak Pies

PREP & COOK 1 HOUR

600g butternut pumpkin, peeled, cut into 3cm pieces
300g cauliflower florets
2 medium zucchini (400g), halved, cut into 2cm pieces
1 red onion, cut into 2cm wedges
2 tblsps olive oil
½ cup frozen peas
4 sheets frozen puff pastry, just thawed
1 egg, lightly beaten
¼ cup tomato pesto

CHEESE SAUCE

80g butter, chopped
⅓ cup plain flour
2 cups milk
1½ cups grated Tasty cheese

1 Grease six oval pie dishes (base measure 7.5cm). Place dishes on an oven tray.

2 Line a large, oven tray with baking paper. Place pumpkin, cauliflower, zucchini and onion on tray. Drizzle over oil. Season with salt and pepper. Toss to combine.

3 Cook in a moderately hot oven (200C) for 25 minutes, or until tender. Transfer to a bowl. Stir in peas. Cool slightly.

4 Meanwhile make cheese sauce, melt butter in a medium saucepan over a medium heat. Add flour. Cook, stirring, for 1 minute. Whisk in milk. Cook, whisking until boiling and thickened. Season. Stir in 1 cup of cheese.

5 Cut three pastry sheets in half diagonally. Line pie dishes with pastry. Trim edges, reserving pastry scraps. Brush edges with egg. Spread tomato pesto over pastry bases.

6 Spoon vegetables into pastry cases. Spoon over warm sauce. Cut remaining pastry sheet into 24 rectangles. Arrange pastry rectangles and some of the reserved pastry scraps over cheese sauce. Brush with egg. Sprinkle with remaining cheese.

7 Cook in a moderately hot oven (200C) for 25 minutes, or until golden. Stand for 5 minutes. Remove from dishes. Serve.

SERVES 6

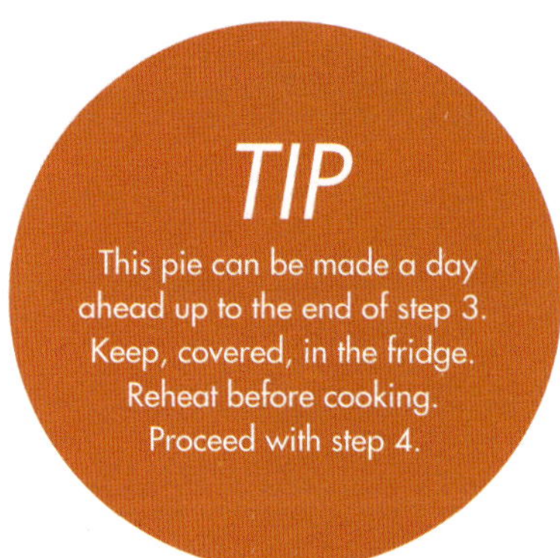

Chicken Chassuer Shepherd's Pie

PREP & COOK 55 MINS

1kg chicken thigh fillets, trimmed, cut into 3cm pieces
300g button mushrooms, halved
1 medium onion, chopped
2 bacon rashers, rind removed, chopped
2 cloves garlic, crushed
2 tblsps plain flour
2 tblsps tomato paste
1½ cups chicken stock
400g can chopped tomatoes
3 tsps fresh thyme leaves, plus extra to garnish

POTATO TOPPING

1.2kg washed potatoes, peeled, chopped
⅓ cup milk
50g butter, chopped

1 Heat an oiled, flameproof casserole dish (10-cup capacity) over a medium to high heat. Cook chicken in two batches, stirring occasionally, for about 5 minutes, or until golden. Remove.

2 Heat same well-oiled dish, add mushrooms, onion, bacon and garlic. Cook, stirring for about 3 minutes, until onion is soft.

3 Add flour and paste. Cook, stirring for 1 minute. Stir in stock, tomatoes and thyme. Bring to boil. Return chicken to pan. Season with salt and pepper. Simmer, covered, stirring occasionally, for 5 minutes. Uncover, simmer for a further 10 minutes, or until thickened. Remove from heat.

4 Meanwhile, to make topping, boil potatoes in a large saucepan of water until tender. Drain. Mash until smooth. Stir in milk and butter. Season with salt and pepper. Spoon over chicken mixture. Spray with cooking oil.

5 Cook in a moderately hot oven (200C) for about 20 minutes, or until golden brown. Stand for 5 minutes.

6 Serve garnished with extra thyme.

SERVES 4

Chicken Paprika

PREP & COOK 1 HOUR

1kg chicken thigh fillets, trimmed, halved
2 tblsps Hungarian sweet paprika
500g jar Roasted Garlic Pasta Sauce with Chunky Tomato & Onion
300g button mushrooms
1 chicken stock cube, crumbled
½ cup sour cream
Cooked pasta and chopped fresh parsley, to serve

1 Heat an oiled, large, deep, non-stick frying pan over a medium to high heat. Add chicken in two batches. Cook for 2 to 3 minutes on each side, or until browned. Remove.

2 Return all the chicken to pan. Sprinkle over paprika. Cook, stirring, until chicken is well coated.

3 Stir in pasta sauce, mushrooms, stock cube and 1 cup water. Season with salt and pepper. Bring to boil. Cover with lid. Gently boil for 20 minutes. Remove lid.

4 Simmer, uncovered, stirring occasionally, for a further 10 minutes, or until chicken is cooked and sauce is slightly thickened. Remove from heat. Stir in sour cream.

5 Serve with pasta and parsley.

SERVES 4

Chicken and Capsicum Tagine

PREP & COOK 40 MINS

600g chicken thigh fillets, chopped
1 large red onion, halved, coarsely chopped
1 large red capsicum, cut into 2cm-wide strips
1 tblsp ground paprika
2 tsps ground cumin
400g jar tomato passata sauce
400g can chickpeas, drained, rinsed
⅓ cup raisins
1 tblsp honey
1 chicken stock cube, crumbled
½ cup chopped fresh coriander, plus extra leaves to garnish
Cooked couscous and crusty bread, to serve

1 Heat a lightly oiled, large, deep, non-stick frying pan over a medium to high heat. Add chicken. Cook, turning occasionally for 6 to 8 minutes, or until evenly browned. Add onion and capsicum. Cook, stirring, for a further 2 minutes.

2 Stir in spices to coat chicken and vegetables.

3 Stir in passata, chickpeas, raisins, honey, stock cube and 1½ cups water. Bring to boil. Gently boil for about 15 minutes, or until slightly thickened and chicken is cooked. Season with salt and pepper. Stir in coriander.

4 Serve with couscous and bread. Garnish with coriander leaves.

SERVES 4

Guiness Beef Stew

PREP & COOK 2 HOURS

1kg beef chuck steak, trimmed, cut into 3cm pieces
500g pickling onions, peeled
⅓ cup tomato paste
440ml can Guinness Stout
1½ cups beef stock
2 tblsps honey
Mashed potato and steamed green beans, to serve

1 Heat an oiled stockpot over a medium to high heat. Add beef in three batches. Cook, turning occasionally, for 3 to 5 minutes, until well browned. Remove.

2 Add onions to same oiled stockpot. Cook, stirring, for 5 minutes, or until lightly browned. Add paste. Cook, stirring, for a further 1 minute.

3 Stir in stout. Bring to boil. Boil 2 minutes. Return beef and meat juices to pot. Stir in stock and honey. Season with salt and pepper. Reduce heat. Cover with lid. Simmer for 1 hour. Uncover and simmer for a further 30 to 40 minutes, until beef is tender and sauce has thickened.

4 Serve with mashed potato and steamed green beans (optional).

SERVES 6

Family Favourite Bolognese Bake

PREP & COOK 1 HOUR

1 onion, finely chopped
1kg lean beef mince
785g jar Bolognese pasta sauce
410g can crushed tomatoes
3 tsps dried Italian herbs
Dressed salad leaves, to serve

TOPPING

300g fusilli pasta
2 cups milk
2 x 29g sachets White Sauce mix (see Tip)
150g packet Perfect Melt 4 Cheeses (see Tip)

1 Grease a large ovenproof dish (12-cup capacity).

2 Heat a lightly oiled, large, deep frying pan over a high heat. Add onion. Cook, stirring, for about 3 minutes, or until soft. Add beef. Cook, stirring to break up mince, for about 10 minutes, or until well browned.

3 Stir in sauce, tomatoes, herbs and ½ cup water. Season with salt and pepper. Bring to boil. Gently boil, stirring occasionally, for about 10 minutes, or until thick. Transfer to prepared dish.

4 Meanwhile, make topping. Cook pasta in a large saucepan of boiling, salted water until tender. Drain.

5 Whisk milk and sauce mixes in same saucepan over a high heat until boiling. Gently boil, whisking constantly for about 2 minutes, or until thickened. Return pasta to pan. Stir to combine. Season with pepper. Spoon topping over beef mixture. Spread evenly. Sprinkle with cheese.

6 Cook in a moderately hot oven (200C) for 20 to 25 minutes, or until golden.

7 Serve bake with dressed salad leaves.

SERVES 4

Beef and Mushroom Hot Chip Bake

PREP & COOK 45 MINS

TIP

For a change, steak cut fries can be replaced with shoestring fries, if preferred. To dress rocket leaves, drizzle over combined olive oil and lemon juice, seasoned with salt and pepper or your favourite store-bought dressing.

900g bag frozen steak cut fries
1 cup grated Perfect Bakes cheese (see Tip)
Dressed rocket leaves, to serve (see tip)

FILLING

2 tblsps olive oil
1 brown onion, finely chopped
200g punnet sliced mushrooms
500g beef mince
2 tblsps tomato paste
2 tblsps traditional gravy powder
1 tblsp Worcestershire sauce
2 cups beef stock
1 cup frozen peas

1 Heat oil in a large, deep frying pan over medium heat. Add onion and mushrooms. Cook, stirring occasionally, for 3 minutes, or until mushrooms are tender. Add beef. Cook over a high heat, stirring to break up mince, for about 4 minutes, or until changed in colour. Stir in paste.

2 Stir gravy powder and Worcestershire sauce into stock. Add to pan and stir to combine. Bring to boil. Gently boil, stirring occasionally, for 10 minutes, or until thickened slightly. Stir in peas. Season with salt and pepper. Remove from heat.

3 Meanwhile, place fries, in a single layer, on a baking paper-lined large oven tray.

4 Cook in a hot oven (220C) for about 20 minutes, or until golden brown. Remove. Season with salt and pepper.

5 Transfer beef mixture to a greased ovenproof dish (10-cup capacity). Arrange fries over top, slightly overlapping. Sprinkle with cheese.

6 Cook in same very hot oven for 8 to 10 minutes, or until top is golden brown. Remove.

7 Serve bake with dressed rocket.

SERVES 4

Chipotle Beef Stew

PREP & COOK 1 HOUR, 40 MINS

700g beef chuck steak, trimmed, cut into 3cm cubes
30g packet taco spice mix
1 red onion, thinly sliced
2 cloves garlic, crushed
400g can diced tomatoes
1 cup beef stock
¼ cup chipotle sauce
400g can black beans, drained, rinsed
½ cup chopped fresh coriander leaves and stems, plus extra leaves to serve
Cooked brown rice, sour cream, sliced avocado and lime wedges, to serve

1 Combine beef and spice mix in a large bowl.

2 Heat an oiled, heavy-based stockpot over a high heat. Add beef in two batches. Cook, stirring occasionally, for about 5 minutes, or until beef is lightly browned. Remove.

3 Heat same oiled pot. Add onion and garlic. Cook, stirring until soft. Return beef to pot.

4 Add tomatoes, stock and sauce. Bring to boil. Gently boil, covered, stirring occasionally for 1 hour. Uncover. Cook for a further 20 minutes, or until beef is tender and sauce is thickened. Add beans. Stir until hot. Stir in coriander.

5 Serve stew with rice, sour cream, avocado, extra coriander and lime wedges.

SERVES 4

Greek Chicken Meatball Bake

PREP & COOK 1 HOUR, 10 MINS

⅓ cup olive oil
2 tblsps tomato paste
6 finger eggplant (600g), cut into 2cm-thick slices
2 capsicum (1 red, 1 yellow), cut into 3cm pieces
1 large red onion, cut into 2cm-thick wedges
Tzatziki dip, lemon wedges and micro herbs (optional), to serve

MEATBALLS

2 thick slices sourdough bread (100g), torn into small pieces
½ cup milk
500g chicken mince
3 cloves garlic, crushed
2 tsps smoked paprika
2 tsps dried oregano

1 Combine 2 tblsps of oil and the paste in a small bowl. Set aside.

2 Place eggplant, capsicum and onion in a roasting pan. Drizzle over remaining oil. Season with salt and pepper. Toss to combine.

3 Cook in a hot oven (220C) for about 25 minutes, stirring halfway through. Remove from oven.

4 Meanwhile, to make meatballs, combine bread and milk in a large bowl. Stand for 10 minutes to soak. Add remaining ingredients. Season. Mix well. Using wetted hands, divide and roll mixture into eight meatballs.

5 Arrange meatballs over vegetables. Brush with tomato paste mixture.

6 Reduce oven to moderately hot (200C). Return pan to oven. Cook for a further 25 minutes, or until meatballs are cooked through.

7 Serve with dip and lemon wedges. Garnish with herbs (optional).

SERVES 4

Creamy Bacon and Zucchini Pasta

PREP & COOK 25 MINS

375g packet fresh lasagne sheets
200g shortcut bacon, chopped
2 medium zucchini (300g), thinly sliced
1 red onion, chopped
2 cloves garlic, crushed
500ml carton vegetable stock
300ml carton pure cream
100g baby spinach leaves
Grated parmesan, to serve

1 Using kitchen scissors, cut lasagne sheets into 4cm-thick strips.

2 Heat an oiled, large, deep frying pan over medium to high heat. Add bacon, zucchini, onion, and garlic. Cook, stirring occasionally for about 6 minutes, or until bacon and zucchini are lightly browned.

3 Pour stock and cream into pan. Season with salt and pepper. Bring to boil. Add pasta strips. Gently stir to combine. Reduce heat. Gently boil, stirring occasionally for about 5 minutes, or until pasta is cooked and sauce is slightly thickened. Stir in spinach leaves until just wilted.

4 Serve pasta topped with parmesan.

SERVES 4-6

Chipotle Chicken

PREP & COOK 1 HOUR, 30 MINS

1 bunch fresh coriander, washed, trimmed
8 chicken thigh fillets (1.5kg), trimmed, halved
1 red onion, chopped
2 cloves garlic, crushed
1 tblsp smoked paprika
2 x 410g cans crushed tomatoes
330g jar roasted whole red peppers, drained, chopped
2 corn cobs, husks removed, cut into 5cm pieces
¼ cup chipotle sauce
Greek yoghurt and corn chips, to serve

1 Finely chop coriander stems. You will need ¼ cup. Set aside some leaves to garnish.

2 Heat a lightly oiled, large flameproof casserole dish (16-cup capacity) over a medium to high heat. Add chicken in two batches. Cook for about 3 minutes on each side, or until browned. Remove.

3 Add onion, garlic and coriander stem. Cook, stirring occasionally until soft. Add paprika. Cook, stirring for 1 minute. Stir in tomatoes, peppers, corn and sauce. Return chicken. Season with salt and pepper. Bring to boil. Cover with lid.

4 Cook in a moderately slow oven (160C) for about 1 hour, or until chicken is cooked.

5 Serve with yoghurt and corn chips. Garnish with coriander leaves.

SERVES 6

Creamy Spinach and Ricotta Cannelloni Bake

PREP & COOK 1 HOUR, 10 MINS

2 x 250g boxes frozen spinach, thawed
500g fresh ricotta
1¼ cups grated Perfect Bakes 3 Cheeses
80g tube fresh Italian Herbs Paste
4 fresh lasagne sheets (see Tip)
490g jar Creamy Carbonara Pasta Sauce
Mix salad leaves, to serve

1 Grease a rectangular ovenproof dish (10-cup capacity).

2 Place spinach in a large sieve. Squeeze to remove excess liquid. Transfer to a large bowl with ricotta, ⅔ cup of the cheese and paste. Season with salt and pepper. Mix well.

3 Place spinach mixture (about 1 cup) lengthways along one long side of each lasagne sheet. Roll up from long sides to enclose filling and make cannelloni. Spread ½ cup of the pasta sauce over base of prepared dish. Arrange cannelloni in a single layer over pasta sauce. Pour over remaining pasta sauce to cover cannelloni. Sprinkle with remaining cheese. Cover with oiled foil.

4 Cook in a moderate oven (180C) for 20 minutes. Remove foil. Cook for a further 30 minutes, or until cannelloni is tender and top is golden brown.

5 Serve with mixed salad leaves.

ECOLOGY

SERVES 4

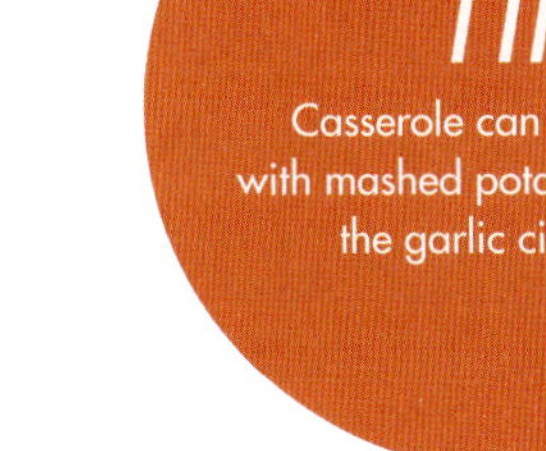

TIP

Casserole can be topped with mashed potato instead of the garlic ciabatta.

French Onion Chicken Casserole

PREP & COOK 1 HOUR, 25 MINS

1.2 kg chicken thigh fillets, trimmed, cut into 3cm pieces
1 large onion, finely chopped
4 carrots (400g), thickly sliced diagonally
2 large stalks celery, sliced
200g button mushrooms
¼ cup cornflour
2 tblsps tomato paste
1 tblsp fresh thyme leaves, plus sprigs to garnish
40g sachet French onion soup mix
2 cups chicken stock
330g packet garlic ciabatta, torn into large pieces
½ cup grated mozzarella cheese

1 Heat an oiled stockpot. Add chicken in two batches. Cook, turning occasionally, about 5 minutes, until browned. Remove.

2 Heat same oiled stockpot. Add onion, carrots, celery and mushrooms. Cook, stirring occasionally, for about 10 minutes, until lightly browned. Return chicken to stockpot.

3 Blend cornflour with ¼ cup water in a jug until smooth. Stir into stockpot with tomato paste, thyme, soup mix and stock. Season with pepper. Bring to boil. Transfer to an ovenproof dish (14-cup capacity). Cover tightly with foil.

4 Cook in a moderately slow oven (160C) for 35 minutes, or until chicken is tender. Remove from oven. Increase oven temperature to moderately hot (200C).

5 Uncover and stir casserole. Scatter ciabatta over top. Spray with olive oil. Sprinkle over cheese.

6 Return to oven. Cook for 10 minutes, or until ciabatta is crisp and cheese is melted.

7 Serve garnished with thyme sprigs.

SERVES 4-6

Massaman Lamb Shank Curry

PREP & COOK 3 HOURS, 45 MINS

6 lamb shanks (2.5kg)
2 brown onions, thinly sliced
½ cup massaman curry paste
2 x 270ml cans coconut milk
1 large beef stock cube, crumbled
800g brushed potatoes, peeled, cut into 5cm pieces
2 tblsps fish sauce
1 tblsp lime juice
Cooked Jasmine rice, green beans, lime wedges and fresh coriander sprigs, to serve

1 Heat an oiled, large flameproof casserole dish (24-cup capacity) over a medium-high heat. Add lamb shanks in two batches. Cook for about 5 minutes, turning regularly, or until browned all over. Remove.

2 Add onions. Cook, stirring occasionally over medium heat, for 5 minutes, or until soft. Add curry paste and cook, stirring for 1 minute. Return lamb. Add coconut milk, stock cube and 1½ cups water. Bring to boil. Cover with lid.

3 Cook in a slow oven (150C) for 2 hours, turning lamb halfway through. Add potatoes. Return to same slow oven. Cook for a further 1 hour, or until lamb is tender enough to fall away from the bone. Remove from oven.

4 Remove lamb from dish. Skim excess fat from top of the sauce. Bring to boil. Gently boil for about 10 minutes, or until thickened slightly. Stir in sauce and juice.

5 Serve lamb with rice, beans and lime wedges. Garnish with coriander.

SERVES 4

Mexican Chicken and Corn Soup

PREP & COOK 30 MINS

1 onion, finely chopped
1 red capsicum, chopped
1-2 tsps Mexican Chilli Spice Blend
1 litre (4 cups) chicken stock
410g can crushed tomatoes
300g jar mild chunky salsa
420g can corn kernels, drained
400g shredded roast chicken meat (see Tip)
Tortilla strips and fresh coriander leaves, to serve

1 Heat an oiled stockpot over a high heat. Add onion and capsicum. Cook, stirring occasionally, for about 3 minutes, or until onion is soft.

2 Add spice blend. Cook, stirring for 1 minute, or until fragrant.

3 Stir in stock, tomatoes and salsa. Bring to boil. Gently boil, uncovered, stirring occasionally for about 10 minutes. Stir in corn and chicken. Gently boil for a further 2 minutes, or until corn and chicken are hot.

4 Serve soup topped with tortilla strips and coriander.

SERVES 6

TIP

Pastitsio can be made to the end of step 4, a day ahead. Keep, covered, in the fridge. Cook in oven, covered with foil, for 45 minutes. Remove foil and cook for a further 15 minutes.

Pastitsio

PREP & COOK 1 HOUR

300g penne rigate pasta
1 large onion, finely chopped
500g beef mince
2 tsps ground cinnamon
700g jar passata sauce
2 tblsps chopped fresh Greek basil, plus leaves to garnish
200g baby spinach leaves

CHEESE SAUCE

100g butter, chopped
⅓ cup plain flour
2½ cups hot milk
1½ cups grated Perfect Bakes 3 Cheeses
2 eggs, lightly beaten

1 Cook pasta in a large saucepan of boiling, salted water until tender. Drain. Return to pan.

2 Meanwhile, heat an oiled, large frying pan over a medium to high heat. Add onion. Cook, stirring occasionally, until soft. Add mince and cinnamon. Cook, stirring to break up mince, for about 5 minutes, or until browned. Add passata sauce, basil and ½ cup water. Simmer, stirring occasionally, for about 10 minutes, or until slightly thickened. Season with salt and pepper.

3 To make cheese sauce, melt butter in a medium saucepan. Add flour. Cook, stirring for 1 minute. Slowly whisk in milk until smooth. Continue to whisk until boiling and thickened. Whisk in 1 cup of the cheese, then eggs. Season with salt and pepper.

4 Stir cheese sauce into pasta. Place half the mixture into a greased ovenproof dish (10-cup capacity). Scatter with half the spinach. Spoon over meat sauce. Scatter with remaining spinach. Top with remaining pasta mixture. Sprinkle with remaining cheese.

5 Cook in a moderate oven (180C) for about 35 minutes, or until the top is golden brown.

6 Serve garnished with basil leaves

SERVES 4

Roast Honey Chilli Chicken and Sweet Potato

PREP & COOK 50 MINS

- 3 medium sweet potatoes (1kg), cut into 2cm-thick slices
- 2 red onions, cut into 3cm wedges
- 2 tblsps olive oil
- 6 chicken thigh cutlets (1.4kg), skin on
- 2 tblsps honey
- 2 tsps bottled freshly chopped chilli
- Steamed broccolini, to serve

1 Toss sweet potatoes and onions in oil in a large roasting pan. Arrange chicken over vegetables. Season with salt and pepper.

2 Cook in a moderately hot oven (200C) for 30 minutes. Remove from oven. Combine honey, chilli and ¼ cup water in a small jug. Drizzle over chicken and vegetables.

3 Return pan to oven. Cook for a further 15 minutes, or until sweet potatoes are tender and chicken is cooked.

4 Serve with broccolini.

SERVES 6

TIP

Diced lamb is available from the refrigerated meat section of major supermarkets. Alternatively, ask your butcher to prepare it for you. We used Patak's Korma Simmer Sauce but you can use any Indian-style simmer sauce.

Lamb, Sweet Potato and Eggplant Korma

PREP & COOK 2 HOURS, 10 MINS

750g diced lamb
2 onions, chopped
450g jar Korma Simmer Sauce (see Tip)
1 sweet potato (400g), peeled, cut into 4cm pieces
1 large eggplant (500g), cut into 2cm pieces
½ cup coarsely chopped fresh coriander, plus extra to serve
Steamed rice and naan bread, to serve

1 Heat an oiled, flameproof casserole dish (14-16-cup capacity) over a high heat. Add lamb in two batches. Cook, turning occasionally, for about 5 minutes, or until browned all over. Remove.

2 Add onions to same dish over a medium heat. Cook, stirring occasionally, for about 3 minutes, or until lightly golden. Return lamb and any meat juices to dish with simmer sauce, sweet potato and 1 cup water. Stir to combine. Bring to boil. Cover with a lid.

3 Cook in a moderately slow oven (160C) for 1 hour. Remove from oven. Stir in eggplant. Cover. Return to oven.

4 Cook for a further 45 minutes, or until lamb and vegetables are tender. Gently stir in coriander. Season with salt and pepper.

5 Garnish with extra coriander. Serve with steamed rice and naan bread.

SERVES 4

Peri Peri Chicken and Potato Bake

PREP & COOK 1 HOUR, 25 MINS

600g chat potatoes, quartered
6 chicken thigh cutlets (1.4kg), skin on
½ cup mild peri peri sauce
1 large red capsicum, cut into 2cm pieces
2 zucchini, cut into 2cm pieces
250g punnet cherry tomatoes
Chopped fresh parsley, to serve

1 Place potatoes in a microwave-safe bowl. Cover. Microwave on High (100%) for 5 minutes.

2 Season chicken with salt and pepper.

3 Heat an oiled, large ovenproof frying pan over a high heat. Add chicken in two batches. Cook for about 5 minutes, or until golden. Remove pan from heat. Return all chicken to pan, skin-side up. Drizzle with sauce. Add potatoes and capsicum to pan. Cover with foil.

4 Cook in a moderate oven (180C) for 30 minutes. Remove and discard foil. Add zucchini and tomatoes. Gently toss to combine. Return to oven. Cook for a further 30 to 40 minutes, or until potatoes are tender and chicken is cooked through.

5 Serve scattered with chopped parsley.

SERVES 4

Mexican Pumpkin and Bean Bake

PREP & COOK 55 MINS

2 x 700g butternut pumpkin halves, peeled, deseeded
2 x 420g can Fiery Mexican Style Beanz (see Tip)
½ x 230g packet yellow corn tortilla strips
1 cup grated Tasty cheese
220g tub guacamole
250g punnet cherry tomatoes, halved

1 Cut pumpkin into 2cm pieces. Spread over base of a lightly oiled ovenproof dish (12-cup capacity).

2 Cook in a moderately hot oven (200C) for about 30 minutes, or until pumpkin is tender. Remove from oven.

3 Spoon beans evenly over pumpkin. Scatter tortilla strips over top. Sprinkle with cheese. Return to oven.

4 Cook for about 15 minutes, or until strips are lightly browned and cheese is melted.

5 Serve bake topped with dollops of guacamole and tomatoes. Garnish with cracked pepper.

S

SERVES 4

One Pan Arrabbiata Lasagne

PREP & COOK 1 HOUR, 15 MINS

375g packet fresh lasagne sheets (8 sheets)
375g tub smooth ricotta
1½ cups grated Perfect Melt 4 Cheeses

SAUCE

1 red onion, finely chopped
1 red capsicum, roughly chopped
3 cloves garlic, crushed
500g beef mince
2 tblsps tomato paste
2 x 400g jars basil pasta sauce
¼ cup marinated split green olives with dried chilli in oil
2 tblsps chopped fresh basil, plus leaves to garnish

1 To make sauce, heat an oiled, large, deep ovenproof frying pan (9-cup capacity) over a medium to high heat. Add onion, capsicum and garlic. Cook, stirring, for about 3 minutes, or until onion is soft. Add beef. Cook, stirring to break up mince, for about 5 minutes, or until browned. Stir in paste.

2 Add pasta sauce, olives, basil and 2 cups water. Season with salt and pepper. Bring to boil. Reduce heat. Gently boil, stirring occasionally, for about 10 minutes, or until sauce is slightly thickened. Remove from heat. Transfer to a bowl.

3 Tear lasagne sheets into large pieces. Spread 1 cup meat sauce over same ovenproof frying pan. Arrange a layer of lasagne sheet pieces over sauce. Repeat layering with remaining meat sauce and lasagne sheet pieces, finishing with a layer of lasagne sheet pieces.

4 Combine ricotta and ½ cup of the cheese in a bowl. Season. Spread over lasagne. Sprinkle with remaining cheese.

5 Cook in a moderate oven (180C) for about 40 minutes, or until top is golden and lasagne is tender.

6 Serve garnished with basil leaves.

SERVES 4

Greek Salmon and Vegie Bake

PREP & COOK 45 MINS

3 medium zucchini, halved lengthways, cut into 3cm pieces
1 red capsicum, cut into 3cm pieces
1 large red onion, roughly chopped
4 x 150g skinless, boneless salmon fillets
½ cup arrabbiata pasta sauce
100g Greek feta
Lemon wedges and fresh thyme sprigs, to serve,

1 Combine zucchini, capsicum and onion in an oiled roasting pan. Drizzle with olive oil. Season with salt and pepper. Toss to coat.

2 Cook in a hot oven (220C) for 20 minutes. Remove from oven. Reduce oven temperature to moderately hot (200C).

3 Place salmon over vegetables. Spoon pasta sauce over salmon. Crumble feta over top.

4 Return to oven. Cook for 10 to 15 minutes, or until salmon is cooked to your liking.

5 Serve with lemon wedges and thyme sprigs.

SERVES 4

Cauliflower and Olive Parmigiana Traybake

PREP & COOK 1 HOUR

1 cauliflower (1.2kg)
1½ cups panko breadcrumbs
1 cup grated parmesan
2 tsps dried Italian herbs
2 tsps garlic powder
2 eggs
350g jar Stir-Through Pasta Sauce with Sundried Tomato & Roasted Garlic
⅓ cup pitted Sicilian olives, halved
1½ cups grated pizza cheese
Cooked fries and salad leaves, to serve

1 Trim leaves and base from cauliflower, leaving stem intact. Cut cauliflower vertically into four x 2cm-thick 'steaks'. Use loose florets to join and make 'steaks' if needed, reserve remaining loose florets for another use.

2 Line a large oven tray with baking paper. Spray paper with olive oil.

3 Combine breadcrumbs, parmesan, herbs and garlic powder in a large dish. Season with salt and pepper. Lightly beat eggs in a shallow dish.

4 One at a time, dip both sides and edges of cauliflower 'steaks' in egg, then coat in breadcrumb mixture, pressing on firmly. Transfer to prepared tray. Spray well with olive oil.

5 Cook in a moderately hot oven (200C) for 30 to 35 minutes, or until golden and just tender. Remove.

6 Spoon sauce evenly over cauliflower 'steaks'. Scatter over olives. Sprinkle with pizza cheese.

7 Return to same oven for a further 10 to 15 minutes, or until cheese is light golden.

8 Serve with fries and salad leaves.

SERVES 4

Honey Mustard Pork and Vegie Bake

PREP & COOK 50 MINS

700g sweet potatoes, cut into 2cm-thick wedges
2 red onions, cut into 2cm-thick wedges
2 tblsps olive oil
4 x 200g pork loin cutlets
2 bunches broccolini, thick stems halved lengthways
250g punnet cherry tomatoes
⅓ cup honey
2 tblsps wholegrain mustard
2 tblsps fresh thyme leaves

1 Place sweet potato and onion in a large, non-stick roasting pan. Drizzle over 1 tblsp oil. Season with salt and pepper. Toss to coat. Spread in an even layer.

2 Cook in a moderately hot oven (200C) for 20 minutes. Remove.

3 Meanwhile, heat a lightly oiled, large, non-stick frying pan over a medium high heat. Add pork. Cook for about 2 minutes on each side, or until golden. Remove.

4 Place broccolini and tomatoes in a large bowl. Add remaining oil. Toss to coat.

5 Combine honey, mustard, thyme and 2 tblsps hot water in a small jug.

6 Place pork over sweet potato and onion in roasting pan. Top with broccolini and tomatoes. Drizzle over honey mixture. Season with salt and pepper.

7 Return pan to same oven. Cook for a further 12 to 15 minutes, or until pork is cooked and vegetables are tender. Serve.

SERVES 4

Honey Soy Pork Hotpot

PREP & COOK 1 HOUR, 10 MINS

750g pork scotch fillet steaks, trimmed, cut into 3cm pieces
200g pouch Honey & Soy Stir-Fry Sauce (see Tip)
1 tblsp fresh ginger paste
6 green spring onions, thinly sliced
2 large carrots, sliced diagonally
150g snow peas, trimmed
Steamed rice and toasted sesame seeds, to serve

1 Heat an oiled stockpot over a medium to high heat. Add pork in two batches. Cook, turning occasionally, for about 5 minutes, or until browned. Remove.

2 Whisk stir-fry sauce with ginger paste and 1½ cups hot water in a jug until combined.

3 Return all pork to stockpot with sauce mixture, onions and carrots. Stir to combine. Bring to boil. Cover with lid. Reduce heat. Simmer, covered, for 35 minutes, stirring occasionally, until pork is tender. Remove lid. Simmer, uncovered for a further 15 minutes, or until sauce is slightly thickened.

4 Stir in snow peas. Cook for a further 2 minutes, or until snow peas are just tender.

5 Serve with steamed rice. Garnish with sesame seeds.

SERVES 8

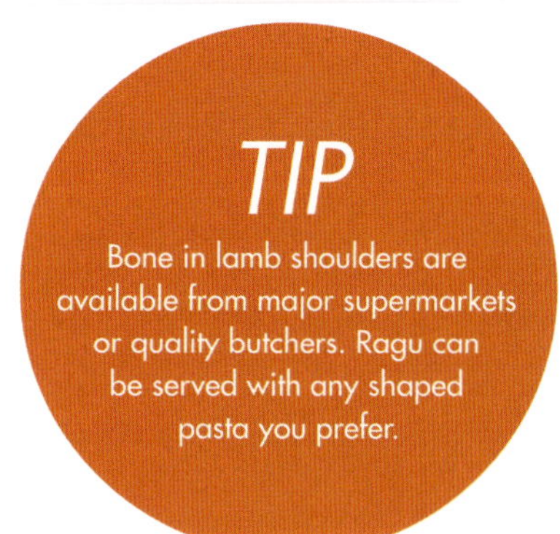

Slow Cooked Lamb Ragu

PREP & COOK 4 HOURS, 30 MINS

2kg lamb shoulder, bone-in
2 carrots, peeled, finely chopped
1 large brown onion, finely chopped
2 cloves garlic, crushed
1 tblsp fresh thyme leaves
½ cup dry red wine
2 tblsps tomato paste
700g jar passata sauce
1½ cups chicken stock
½ cup chopped fresh parsley
Cooked pappardelle and finely grated parmesan, to serve

1 Season lamb with salt and pepper.

2 Heat an oiled, large, flameproof casserole dish (16-cup capacity) over medium-high heat. Add lamb. Cook for about 5 minutes on each side, or until browned. Remove.

3 Add carrot, onion, garlic and thyme. Cook, stirring occasionally, for 5 minutes, or until soft. Add wine. Bring to boil. Boil for 1 minute.

4 Stir in tomato paste. Add passata and stock. Return lamb skin-side up. Bring to boil. Cover with a piece of baking paper and a tight-fitting lid.

5 Cook in a slow oven (150C) for about 4 hours, or until lamb is falling away from the bone. Remove. Transfer lamb to a clean board. Shred into pieces, discarding bones. Return lamb to sauce in dish. Stir in parsley. Season with salt and pepper.

6 Serve with pappardelle and parmesan.

SERVES 4

TIP

Make and puree soup up to three days ahead. Keep covered in the fridge. Soup can also be kept in freezer in containers for up to one month.

Pumpkin Soup with Crispy Chorizo

PREP & COOK 45 MINS

1.25kg butternut pumpkin
1 large onion, finely chopped
2 cloves garlic, crushed
1½ tsps sweet smoked paprika
1 litre (4 cups) chicken stock
1 chorizo (130g), finely chopped
Sour cream, to serve

1 Peel and deseed pumpkin. Cut into 3cm pieces.

2 Heat an oiled stockpot over a medium heat. Add onion, garlic and paprika. Cook, stirring occasionally for about 3 minutes, or until soft.

3 Add stock, 1 cup water and pumpkin to pot. Season with salt and pepper. Bring to boil. Gently boil, uncovered, stirring occasionally, for about 25 minutes, or until pumpkin is very tender. Remove from heat. Cool slightly.

4 Meanwhile, heat a small non-stick frying pan over a medium heat. Add chorizo. Cook, stirring for about 5 minutes, or until crisp. Drain on absorbent kitchen paper.

5 Blend soup, in two batches in a blender until smooth. Return soup to stockpot. Stir over a low heat until hot.

6 Divide soup among serving bowls. Serve with sour cream and chorizo. Season.

SERVES 4

Pork and Prawn Short and Long Soup

PREP & COOK 30 MINS

200g packet thin dried egg noodles
1 cup sliced, dried shitake mushrooms (20g)
¼ cup soy sauce
1 tblsp Chinese cooking wine
1 bunch gai lan (Chinese broccoli) (250g)
2 litres (8 cups) chicken stock
355g packet pork and prawn wontons
4 green spring onions, thinly sliced
Chilli oil, to serve

1 Cook noodles in a large saucepan of boiling, salted water until tender. Drain. Refresh under cold water. Drain well.

2 Meanwhile, place mushrooms in a large heatproof bowl. Cover with 1 cup boiling water. Stand for about 5 minutes, or until soft. Stir in sauce and cooking wine.

3 Trim gai lan. Cut off stems. Thinly slice stems crossways and coarsely chop leaves, keeping them separate.

4 Place stock and mushroom mixture in a stockpot. Bring to boil. Add wontons and gai lan stems. Return to boil. Gently boil, uncovered for about 3 minutes, or until wontons are cooked. Stir in the gai lan leaves and half the onions. Cook, stirring for 1 minute.

5 Divide noodles among serving bowls. Spoon over soup. Garnish with remaining onions. Serve with chilli oil.

SERVES 4-6

Mac 'n' Cheese Tuna Bake

PREP & COOK 1 HOUR

200g pasta curls
425g can tuna in springwater, drained
1½ cups frozen peas, thawed
1¼ cups grated Tasty cheese
2 x 500g jars Pasta Bake with Three Cheese Sauce
2 thick slices white bread, torn into pieces

1 Cook pasta in a large saucepan of boiling water until tender. Drain. Transfer to a lightly greased, large ovenproof dish (12-cup capacity).

2 Flake tuna over pasta. Scatter over peas and ¾ cup cheese.

3 Place pasta sauces and ¼ cup water in a large saucepan. Stir over medium to high heat until combined and hot. Pour evenly over ingredients in dish.

4 Sprinkle combined bread and remaining cheese over top. Lightly spray with cooking oil.

5 Cook in a moderate oven (180C) for about 45 minutes, or until topping is crisp and golden brown. Serve.

SERVES 4

Tuscan Roast Chicken and Vegies

PREP & COOK 1 HOUR, 10 MINS

4 chicken thigh cutlets (1.2kg), skin on
750g baby chat potatoes, halved
1 head garlic, halved
2 tblsps Tuscan seasoning
2 tsps finely grated lemon rind
2 tblsps olive oil
800g Kent pumpkin, seeds removed, cut into thin wedges
3 medium zucchini, halved lengthways, cut into 4cm lengths
Steamed green beans and charred lemon halves, to serve

1 Place chicken, potatoes and garlic in a large roasting pan. Sprinkle with seasoning and rind. Drizzle over oil. Season with pepper. Toss to coat. Spread in an even layer, placing chicken skin-side up.

2 Cook in a moderately hot oven (200C) for 30 minutes.

3 Remove roasting pan from oven. Turn potatoes over. Add pumpkin and zucchini, turning to coat in pan juices. Cook for a further 25 to 30 minutes, or until chicken is cooked and vegetables are tender.

4 Serve with steamed beans and lemon halves.

TIP

Lamb shoulders vary in size. To serve 6-8 people, use two smaller shoulders (about 1.3kg each). Swap red-skinned potatoes for baby chats and red wine with extra stock, if preferred.

SERVES 4-6

Slow-Roasted Lamb Shoulder with Smashed Potatoes

PREP & COOK 3 HOURS, 40 MINS

1.8kg lamb shoulder, bone in, shank attached
1 small bunch fresh rosemary
2 onions, cut into wedges (no need to peel)
1 head garlic, halved
Steamed green beans and broccolini, to serve

SMASHED POTATOES

1 kg small red-skinned potatoes (see Tip)
2 tblsps olive oil

GRAVY

2 tblsps plain flour
2 cups beef stock
⅓ cup red wine

1 Using tip of a sharp knife, make small incisions across top of lamb. Insert small sprigs of rosemary into each incision. Reserve sprigs to garnish. Scatter onions, garlic and remaining rosemary sprigs over base of an oiled, large roasting pan. Place lamb in pan, skin-side up. Season with salt and pepper. Pour 1 cup water into pan. Cover tightly with foil.

2 Cook in a slow oven (150C) for 3 hours. Remove and uncover. Increase oven temperature to hot (220C). Return lamb to oven. Cook for about 20 minutes, or until top is browned. Transfer lamb to a large plate. Cover with foil and a clean tea towel. Stand 20 minutes.

3 While lamb is cooking, prepare smashed potatoes. Boil potatoes in a large saucepan of boiling water for about 10 minutes, until almost tender (don't overcook). Drain. Transfer to an oven tray lined with baking paper. Flatten with the back of a spoon. Drizzle with oil. Season with salt and pepper.

4 Cook in a hot oven (220C) for about 30 minutes, or until potatoes are crisp.

5 To make gravy, reserve 2 tblsps pan juices in roasting pan. Place pan over a medium to high heat. Add flour. Cook, stirring for 2 minutes, scraping up any crispy bits from base of pan. Reduce heat. Gradually, stir in stock and wine. Simmer, stirring, for about 5 minutes until thickened. Strain through sieve into a large jug.

6 Serve lamb with smashed potatoes, gravy and steamed greens. Garnish with reserved rosemary.

SERVES 6

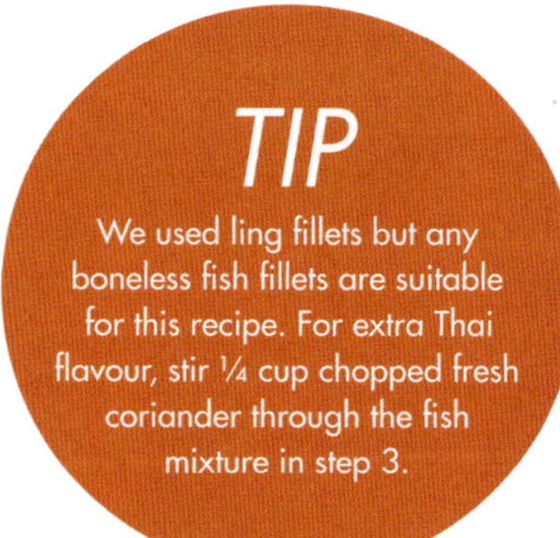

Thai Fish Curry Pie

PREP & COOK 40 MINS

1 small onion, finely chopped
2 tblsps Thai green curry paste
500g sweet potato, cut into 2cm pieces
400ml can coconut milk
2 tsps fish sauce
2 tsps brown sugar
500g skinless, boneless white fish fillets, cut into 3cm pieces
2 tsps plain flour
8 sheets filo pastry
Lime wedges and fresh coriander leaves, to serve

1 Heat a well-oiled, large frying pan over a medium to high heat. Add onion. Cook stirring occasionally until soft. Add paste and sweet potato. Cook, stirring occasionally for 5 minutes.

2 Stir in coconut milk, fish sauce and sugar. Bring to boil. Gently boil for about 10 minutes, stirring occasionally, until sauce is thickened slightly and sweet potato is almost tender.

3 Toss fish in flour. Add to pan. Cook, gently stirring for a further 2 minutes, or until hot. Transfer to a round ovenproof dish (8-cup capacity).

4 Working with one pastry sheet at a time. Spray with cooking oil. Fold in half then loosely scrunch and arrange over fish mixture. Continue with remaining pastry sheets and oil spray. Lightly spray top with cooking oil.

5 Cook in a moderately hot oven (200C) for 10 minutes. Reduce temperature to moderate (180C). Cook for a further 10 to 15 minutes, or until fish is cooked and top is golden. Stand for 5 minutes before serving.

6 Serve with lime wedges. Garnish with coriander.

SERVES 4-6

Creamy Chicken with Sweet Potato and Cauliflower

PREP & COOK 1 HOUR

6 chicken thigh cutlets (1.4kg), skin on
2½ tsps lemon pepper spice blend
450g cauliflower, cut into large florets
450g sweet potato, halved lengthways, cut into 2cm pieces
1 chicken stock cube, crumbled
29g sachet White Sauce mix (see Tip)
1 cup milk
1 tblsp Dijon mustard
1 tblsp fresh thyme leaves, plus extra sprigs to garnish

1 Heat a lightly oiled, deep, flameproof roasting pan over a medium high heat. Sprinkle chicken skin with 1½ tsps of the lemon pepper.

2 Add chicken to pan, skin-side down. Cook for about 5 minutes, or until golden. Turn chicken over. Remove pan from heat.

3 Place cauliflower and sweet potato around chicken in dish. Spray with cooking oil. Sprinkle remaining lemon pepper over chicken and vegetables.

4 Cook in a moderately hot oven (200C) for 25 minutes. Remove from oven.

5 Dissolve stock cube with ¾ cup boiling water in a large heatproof jug. Whisk in white sauce, milk, mustard and thyme until smooth. Pour sauce over chicken and vegetables. Return to same oven.

6 Cook for about 15 minutes, or until sauce is thickened and chicken is cooked.

7 To serve, place chicken and vegetables on serving plates, whisk sauce in pan before spooning over. Garnish with thyme sprigs.

SERVES 6

Red Curry Chicken Pie

PREP & COOK 1 HOUR, 30 MINS

3 sheets frozen puff pastry, just thawed
1 egg, lightly beaten

FILLING

1.4kg chicken thigh fillets, trimmed, cut into 2cm pieces
2 tblsps olive oil
1 large onion, finely chopped
2 cloves garlic, crushed
⅓ cup red curry paste
2 tblsps plain flour
400ml can light coconut milk
1 tblsp fish sauce
½ cup frozen peas
½ cup finely chopped fresh coriander

1 Grease a 24cm loose-base flan tin (3.5cm deep). Place on an oven tray.

2 To make filling, heat an oiled, large, deep frying pan over a high heat. Add chicken in two batches. Cook, stirring occasionally, for about 6 minutes, or until golden brown. Remove.

3 Heat oil in same pan. Add onion and garlic. Cook, stirring, over a medium heat until soft. Stir in paste. Cook, stirring, for a further 1 to 2 minutes, until fragrant. Stir in flour until combined.

4 Return chicken to pan. Stir in coconut milk, sauce and ⅓ cup water. Bring to boil. Gently boil for about 5 minutes, or until chicken is cooked and sauce is thickened. Remove from heat, stir in peas and coriander. Transfer to a heatproof bowl. Refrigerate for 30 minutes, or until cool.

5 To assemble pie, join two pastry sheets together with edges overlapping by 2cm. Use a rolling pin to gently seal joins. Line base and side of tin with pastry, allowing excess to overhang edge. Trim excess pastry and use to fill gaps in pastry case. Press edges to seal.

6 Spoon filling into pastry case. Cut remaining pastry sheet into 16 squares. Arrange over filling. Brush with egg.

7 Cook in a hot oven (220C) for 20 minutes. Reduce temperature to moderately hot (200C). Cook for a further 20 minutes, or until pastry is golden brown, covering loosely with foil if overbrowning. Remove from oven. Stand in tin for 20 minutes. Serve.

SERVES 4

Vegetable Bean Soup with Spicy Capsicum Dip

PREP & COOK 35 MINS

1 leek, trimmed, halved lengthways, thinly sliced
1 large carrot, peeled, cut into 2cm pieces
2 cloves garlic, crushed
2 medium zucchini, halved lengthways, sliced
2 medium potatoes, peeled, cut into 2cm pieces
1 medium sweet potato, peeled, cut into 2cm pieces
1 litre (4 cups) vegetable stock
425g can cannellini beans, drained, rinsed
120g bag baby spinach leaves
Greek yoghurt and crusty bread, to serve

SPICY CAPSICUM DIP

280g jar chargrilled peppers, drained
2 tsps Moroccan Spice Blend
¼ cup olive oil

1 Heat an oiled stockpot over a medium to high heat. Add leek, carrot and garlic. Cook, stirring occasionally, for about 6 to 8 minutes, or until soft.

2 Stir in zucchini, potato, sweet potato, stock and 2 cups water. Season with salt and pepper. Bring to boil. Gently boil, covered, stirring occasionally for about 15 minutes, or until vegetables are tender. Stir in beans. Cook for a further 2 minutes, or until hot. Remove from heat. Stir in spinach until just wilted.

3 Meanwhile, to make dip, process all ingredients in a food processor until smooth. Season with salt. Transfer to a serving bowl.

4 Serve hot soup with dip, yoghurt and crusty bread.

The SWEET STUFF

Whether it's cooked in an oven or a slow cooker, nothing says comfort food quite like dessert.

SERVES 4-6

Berry Caramel Croissant Pudding

PREP & COOK 1 HOUR, 5 MINS

6 x 50g all butter croissants
⅓ cup caramel spread, plus extra to serve
1 cup frozen mixed berries
Vanilla ice-cream, to serve

CUSTARD

2 cups milk
300ml carton pure cream
1 tsp vanilla bean paste
3 eggs
⅓ cup caster sugar

1 Spray a rectangular, ovenproof dish (12-cup capacity) with oil.

2 Cut croissants in half horizontally. Spread caramel over cut sides. Sandwich together. Arrange in a single layer over base of dish. Scatter over berries.

3 To make custard, place milk, cream and vanilla in a microwave-safe jug. Microwave on High (100%) for 2 to 3 minutes, or until warmed. Whisk eggs and sugar in a large jug until combined. Whisk in warmed milk mixture. Pour over croissants in dish.

4 Place dish in a large roasting pan. Pour enough boiling water into roasting pan to come halfway up side of the dish.

5 Cook in a moderately slow oven (160C) for about 40 to 45 minutes, or until custard is set and top is crisp and golden. Remove pan from oven. Transfer dish to a wooden board. Stand for 15 minutes.

6 Drizzle warm pudding with extra warmed caramel. Serve with ice-cream.

SERVES 10-12

Blueberry Custard Cheesecake

PREP & COOK 1 HOUR, 20 MINS

250g packet Custard Cream biscuits
100g unsalted butter, melted
Whipped cream, to serve

FILLING

2 x 250g packets cream cheese, chopped, at room temperature
¾ cup caster sugar
2 tsps vanilla extract
3 eggs
300ml tub thickened cream
¼ cup custard powder
125g punnet blueberries

BLUEBERRY SAUCE

2 cups frozen blueberries
⅓ cup caster sugar

1 Invert base of a 22cm round springform pan (base measures 21cm). Grease and line base with baking paper.

2 Process biscuits in a food processor until finely crushed. Add butter. Process until combined. Press over base and three-quarters of the way up side of prepared pan. Refrigerate while preparing filling.

3 To make filling, process cream cheese, sugar and vanilla in same, clean food processor until smooth. Add eggs, one at a time, processing until combined. Add cream and custard powder. Process until smooth. Pour over biscuit base. Sprinkle with blueberries. Place on an oven tray.

4 Cook in a moderately slow oven (160C) for about 45 minutes, or until just set. Cheesecake should have a slight wobble. Turn oven off. Cool in oven 1 hour with door ajar. Remove from oven. Cover and refrigerate overnight.

5 To make blueberry sauce, combine blueberries, sugar and ⅓ cup water in a medium saucepan over a medium heat. Cook, stirring occasionally until sugar is dissolved. Bring to boil. Gently boil for 3 to 5 minutes, or until slightly thickened. Remove from heat. Cool slightly. Press sauce mixture through a sieve over a heatproof jug.

6 Remove side of pan. Transfer cheesecake to a serving plate. Serve topped with whipped cream and blueberry sauce.

MAKES 8

Cinnamon Apple Pie Cheesecakes

PREP & COOK 45 MINS

385g can apple slices pie fruit, drained
8 slices brioche loaf (see Tip)
Dollop cream and cinnamon sugar, to serve

FILLING

250g block cream cheese, chopped, room temperature
⅓ cup caster sugar
1 tsp vanilla bean extract
½ cup sour cream
1 egg

1 Grease 8-holes of two 6-hole non-stick Texan muffin pans (¾-cup capacity).

2 Place apple slices on a plate lined with absorbent kitchen paper to absorb excess moisture.

3 To make, beat cream cheese, sugar and vanilla in a small bowl with an electric mixer until smooth. Add sour cream and egg. Beat until combined.

4 Using a rolling pin, flatten brioche slices. Press each into a greased pan-hole. Divide apple slices evenly over brioche. Spoon over filling. Tap pan on bench to remove any air bubbles. Smooth tops.

5 Cook in a slow oven (150C) for about 25 minutes, or until firm to touch. Transfer pan to a wire rack to cool for 30 minutes. To remove cheesecakes, run a small knife around inside edge of each hole.

6 To serve, top warm cheesecakes with cream. Dust with cinnamon sugar.

SERVES 8

Double Choc Cheesecake

PREP & COOK 1 HOUR

4 pack (420g) Double Choc Muffins
2 x 250g blocks cream cheese, chopped, at room temperature
⅔ cup caster sugar
2 tsps vanilla extract
⅔ cup sour cream
3 eggs
Whipped cream and cocoa powder, to serve

1 Invert base of a 23cm round springform pan (base measures 22cm). Grease and line base and side with baking paper, extending paper 2cm above pan edge.

2 Crumble three muffins into coarse crumbs. Sprinkle into prepared pan. Press lightly to cover base of pan in an even layer. Place pan on an oven tray.

3 Beat cream cheese, sugar and vanilla in a small bowl with an electric mixer until smooth. Beat in sour cream. Beat in eggs, one at a time, until combined.

4 Dollop half the cream cheese mixture over muffin base in pan. Crumble the remaining muffin into fine crumbs. Sprinkle over cheese mixture. Dollop remaining cream cheese mixture over top. Gently spread to cover.

5 Cook in a moderately slow oven (160C) for about 45 minutes, or until just set. Cheesecake should have a slight wobble. Turn off oven. Cool in oven for 30 minutes with door ajar. Remove from oven. Stand in pan for 30 minutes.

6 Remove side of pan. Transfer cheesecake to a serving plate. Cut into pieces. Top with whipped cream. Dust with sifted cocoa.

SERVES 6

Gingerbread Apple Pie

PREP & COOK 55 MINS

125g unsalted butter, melted
⅓ cup firmly packed brown sugar
1 egg, lightly beaten
1¾ cups self-raising flour
1 tblsp ground ginger
2 tsps ground cinnamon
3 tsps raw sugar
Vanilla ice-cream and warmed caramel spread, to serve

FILLING

770g can apple slices pie fruit, drained
2 tblsps golden syrup
2 tsps finely grated lemon rind

1 Lightly grease a 24cm round loose-based flan tin (2.5cm deep). Place on an oven tray.

2 Whisk butter, brown sugar and egg in a large bowl until combined. Stir in combined flour, ginger and cinnamon to form a dough. Cut two-thirds from the dough, shape into a flat disc. Shape the remaining dough into a smaller flat disc. Wrap both in plastic wrap. Refrigerate pastry discs for 20 minutes.

3 Meanwhile, to make filling, combine all ingredients in a bowl.

4 Roll out the large pastry disc between two sheets baking paper to a 24cm round. Remove top sheet of paper. Invert pastry over tin, then remove other sheet of paper. Press pastry up side of tin. Spoon filling into pastry case. Roll out small pastry disc between two sheets baking paper large enough to cover filling. Remove top sheet of paper. Invert over filling, then remove other sheet of paper. Press edge to seal, trimming if needed. Lightly brush with water. Sprinkle with raw sugar.

5 Cook in a moderate oven (180C) for about 30 minutes, or until pastry is golden brown. Stand pie for 20 minutes before serving.

6 Serve pie with ice-cream. Drizzled over warmed caramel spread.

SERVES 6

Lemon Crisp Apple Berry Crumble

PREP & COOK 55 MINS

4 Granny Smith apples (700g)
4 pink lady apples (700g)
50g unsalted butter, chopped
⅓ cup caster sugar
125g punnet blueberries
Vanilla ice-cream, to serve

TOPPING

6 Lemon Crisp biscuits
½ cup self-raising flour
⅓ cup traditional rolled oats
60g cold unsalted butter, chopped

1 Peel apples. Cut into quarters. Remove and discard cores. Roughly chop.

2 Melt butter in a deep, ovenproof frying pan over a medium-high heat until bubbling. Stir in apples, sugar and ¼ cup water. Stir until sugar is dissolved. Bring to boil. Cover with lid. Simmer, stirring occasionally for about 10 minutes, or until apples are just tender. Stir in blueberries.

3 Meanwhile, to make topping, place biscuits in a snap-lock bag. Lightly crush. Combine flour and oats in a medium bowl. Using your fingertips, rub in butter until mixture resembles crumbs. Stir in crushed biscuits. Sprinkle topping over fruit.

4 Cook in a moderate oven (180C) for 20 to 25 minutes, or until topping is golden brown. Remove from oven. Stand for 10 minutes.

5 Serve crumble with ice-cream.

SERVES 6-8

TIP

This pudding is best served warm. It can be made up to two days ahead. Cover cold pudding in plastic wrap. Store in an airtight container. Reheat to serve. Metal pudding steamers are available from kitchen shops or online.

Slow Cooker Golden Syrup Pudding

PREP & COOK 3 HOURS, 15 MINS

Melted unsalted butter, for greasing
½ cup golden syrup, plus extra to serve
150g unsalted butter, chopped, at room temperature
¾ cup caster sugar
1 tsp finely grated orange rind
2 tsps vanilla extract
3 eggs
1½ cups self-raising flour
⅓ cup milk
Whipped cream, to serve

1 Grease a metal pudding steamer (8-cup capacity) with melted butter. Pour syrup into base of the steamer.

2 Beat butter, sugar, orange rind and vanilla in a small bowl of an electric mixer until light and fluffy. Beat in eggs, one at a time, until combined. Transfer mixture to a large bowl.

3 Add flour and milk. Stir until combined. Spoon into prepared steamer. Smooth over top.

4 Place a piece of baking paper then foil over the top of steamer. Tie firmly with string to secure. Cover with metal lid.

5 Place a small, heat-proof saucer in the centre of a removable bowl of a 5- to 6-litre capacity slow cooker. Sit steamer on the saucer. Pour in enough cold water (about 8 cups) to come three-quarters of the way up the side of steamer. Cover cooker tightly with two sheets of foil. Cover with lid.

6 Cook on HIGH for 3 hours. Remove steamer. Stand for 15 minutes. Remove lid, foil and paper. Turn out pudding onto a serving plate.

7 Drizzle extra golden syrup over warm pudding. Serve with cream.

SERVES 8-10

Slow Cooker Hot Fudge Coconut Pudding

PREP & COOK 2 HOURS, 50 MINS

2 cups self-raising flour
⅓ cup cocoa
½ cup firmly packed brown sugar
1 cup Dark Choc Chips
270ml can coconut milk
100g unsalted butter, melted
2 tsps vanilla bean paste
Vanilla ice-cream, to serve

TOPPING

1½ cups firmly packed brown sugar
½ cup cocoa powder

1 Lightly grease a removable bowl of a 5- to 6-litre capacity slow cooker. Line base and side with baking paper.

2 Sift flour and cocoa into a large bowl. Stir in sugar and Choc Chips.

3 Place coconut milk, butter and vanilla into a jug. Whisk until combined. Add to flour mixture. Stir until smooth. Spoon into prepared bowl. Smooth over top.

4 To make the topping, combine sugar and cocoa in a large jug. Gradually stir in 2½ cups boiling water. Slowly pour over pudding mixture. Cover with lid.

5 Cook on LOW for about 2 hours, or until firm to touch. Stand, covered, for 30 minutes.

6 Serve pudding with ice-cream.

SERVES 10-12

TIP

Before you start, make sure the springform pan fits in your slow cooker. When wrapping the pan in plastic wrap and foil, make sure there are no gaps for water to seep in. Cheesecake can also be served cold.

Slow Cooker Cheesecake with Blueberry Sauce

PREP & COOK 2 HOURS, 55 MINS

½ x 250g packet Butternut Snap Cookie
½ cup oven-roasted almonds
50g unsalted butter, melted
2 x 250g blocks cream cheese, chopped, at room temperature
1 cup caster sugar
2 tsps finely grated lemon rind
3 eggs
250g tub sour cream
2 tblsps plain flour

BLUEBERRY SAUCE

2 cups frozen blueberries
½ cup caster sugar
2 tblsps lemon juice
1 tblsp cornflour

1 Invert base of a 20cm round springform pan (base measures 19cm). Grease and line base and side with baking paper. Cover outside of pan in two layers of plastic wrap, then foil.

2 Process biscuits and almonds in a food processor until finely crushed. Add butter. Process until combined. Press over base of prepared pan. Refrigerate.

3 Process cream cheese, sugar and rind in same, clean food processor until smooth. Add eggs, one at a time, processing until combined. Add sour cream and flour. Process until smooth. Pour mixture over biscuit base.

4 Place a small, heatproof bowl (4cm deep) upside down in the centre of a removable bowl of a 5- to 6-litre slow cooker. Sit the springform pan on the small bowl. Pour enough boiling water (about 5 cups) into the slow cooker bowl, until it touches the base of the springform pan. Cover slow cooker with lid.

5 Cook on HIGH for about 2 hours and 30 minutes, or until set. Remove pan. Stand cheesecake in pan for 30 minutes.

6 Meanwhile, to make blueberry sauce, combine all ingredients in a medium saucepan. Stir over a medium heat until sugar is dissolved. Bring to boil. Gently boil, stirring occasionally, for 3 minutes, or until slightly thickened.

7 Serve warm cheesecake with warm blueberry sauce.

SERVES 8

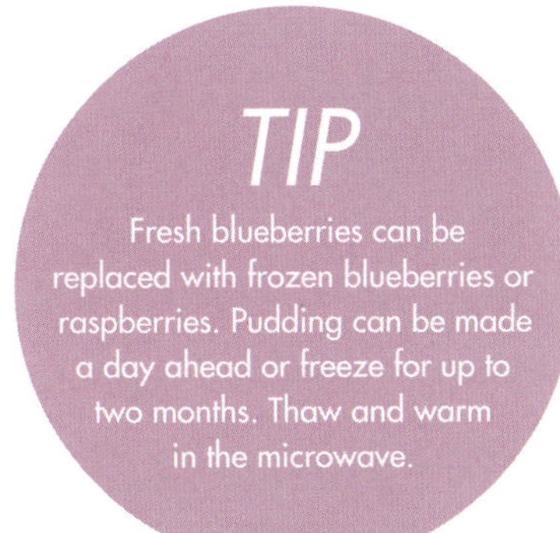

Sticky Date Blueberry Pudding

PREP & COOK 1 HOUR, 15 MINS

1½ cups (250g) pitted dates, chopped
1 tsp bicarbonate of soda
60g unsalted butter, chopped, at room temperature
¾ cup firmly packed brown sugar
2 eggs, at room temperature
1 cup self-raising flour
125g punnet blueberries
Vanilla ice-cream, to serve

CARAMEL SAUCE

1 cup thickened cream
1 cup firmly packed brown sugar

1 Grease a 20cm deep, round cake pan. Line base and side with baking paper.

2 Combine dates and 1¼ cups water in a saucepan. Bring to boil. Remove from heat. Stir in soda. Stand 10 minutes to cool slightly.

3 Beat butter and sugar in a small bowl with an electric mixer until light and fluffy. Beat in eggs, one at a time, until just combined. Stir in date mixture and sifted flour. Mix well. Scatter over half the blueberries. Pour into prepared pan.

4 Cook in a moderate oven (180C) for about 50 minutes, or until skewer inserted into centre of cake comes out clean. Stand in pan for 5 minutes.

5 Meanwhile, to make caramel sauce, combine cream and sugar in a small saucepan over a medium heat. Stir until sugar is dissolved. Bring to boil. Gently boil for about 5 minutes, or until sauce is slightly thickened.

6 Serve pudding with remaining blueberries, warm caramel sauce and ice-cream.

Glossary

BLACK BEANS also called turtle beans or black kidney beans; an earthy-flavoured dried bean (fermented soy beans). Often used in Mexican and South American cooking.

CANNELLINI BEANS small white bean similar in appearance and flavour to other phaseolus vulgaris varieties (great northern, navy or haricot). Available dried or canned.

CASTER SUGAR a finely granulated table sugar; also called superfine sugar.

COCONUT MILK obtained from the second pressing of the white coconut flesh, then diluted with water; the first pressing (without added water) yields coconut cream. Available in cans and cartons from most supermarkets.

CORNFLOUR available made from corn or wheat (wheaten cornflour gives a lighter texture in cakes); used as a thickening agent.

COUSCOUS a dehydrated, grain-like product made from semolina; it swells to three or four times its original size when liquid is added. It is eaten like rice with a tagine, as a side dish or salad ingredient.

CUMIN the dried seed of a plant related to the parsley family. Available dried as seeds or ground. It has a spicy, curry-like flavour.

EGGPLANT also called aubergine. Ranging in size from tiny to very large and in colour from pale green to deep purple. Can be purchased chargrilled, packed in oil, in jars.

FENNEL a white to very pale green-white, firm, crisp, roundish vegetable about 8-12cm in diameter. The bulb has a slightly sweet, anise flavour but the leaves have a much stronger taste.

FISH SAUCE called nam pla (Thai) or nuoc nam (Vietnamese); made from pulverised salted fermented fish, most often anchovies. Has a pungent smell and strong taste, so use sparingly.

GARAM MASALA a blend of spices that includes cardamom, cinnamon, cumin, coriander, cloves and fennel. Black pepper and chilli can be added.

HARISSA a North African paste made from dried red chillies, garlic, olive oil and caraway seeds; can be used as a rub for meat, an ingredient in sauces and dressings, or as a condiment.

PANKO BREADCRUMBS also known as Japanese breadcrumbs. Available in two types: larger pieces and fine crumbs; both have a lighter texture than Western-style crumbs.

PAPRIKA ground, dried, sweet red capsicum; there are many types available, including sweet, hot, mild and smoked.

PASSATA sieved tomato puree; contains no flavourings. Sold alongside bottled pasta sauce.

RICOTTA CHEESE a soft, sweet, moist, white cow-milk cheese with a low fat content and a slightly grainy texture.

TURMERIC also called kamin; is a rhizome related to galangal and ginger. Must be grated or pounded to release its acrid aroma and pungent flavour. Fresh turmeric can be substituted with the more commonly found powder at 1 teaspoon for every 20g fresh.

VANILLA BEAN PASTE made from vanilla bean pods and contains real seeds; 1 teaspoon is equal to a whole vanilla bean.

WORCESTERSHIRE SAUCE thin, dark-brown spicy sauce developed by the British when in India; it is used as a seasoning and as a condiment.

ZUCCHINI also called courgette.

Conversion Chart

MEASURES

One Australian metric measuring cup holds approx 250ml; one Australian metric tablespoon holds 20ml; one Australian metric teaspoon holds 5ml.

The difference between one country's measuring cups and another's is within a 2- or 3-teaspoon variance and will not affect cooking results. North America, New Zealand and the UK use a 15ml tablespoon. All cup and spoon measurements are level.

The most accurate way of measuring dry ingredients is to weigh them.

When measuring liquids, use a clear glass or plastic jug with the metric markings.

We use extra-large eggs with an average weight of 60g each.

DRY MEASURES

metric	imperial
15g	½oz
30g	1oz
60g	2oz
90g	3oz
125g	4oz (¼lb)
155g	5oz
185g	6oz
220g	7oz
250g	8oz (½lb)
280g	9oz
315g	10oz
345g	11oz
375g	12oz (¾lb)
410g	13oz
440g	14oz
470g	15oz
500g	16oz (1lb)
750g	24oz (1½lb)
1kg	32oz (2lb)

LIQUID MEASURES

metric	imperial
30ml	1 fluid oz
60ml	2 fluid oz
100ml	3 fluid oz
125ml	4 fluid oz
150ml	5 fluid oz
190ml	6 fluid oz
250ml	8 fluid oz
300ml	10 fluid oz
500ml	16 fluid oz
600ml	20 fluid oz
1000ml (1 litre)	1¾ pints

LENGTH MEASURES

metric	imperial
3mm	⅛in
6mm	¼in
1cm	½in
2cm	¾in
2.5cm	1in
5cm	2in
6cm	2½in
8cm	3in
10cm	4in
13cm	5in
15cm	6in
18cm	7in
20cm	8in
22cm	9in
25cm	10in
28cm	11in
30cm	12in (1ft)

OVEN TEMPERATURES

The oven temperatures in this book are for conventional ovens; for fan-forced ovens, decrease by 10-20 degrees.

	°C (Celsius)	°F (Fahrenheit)
Very slow	120	250
Slow	150	300
Moderately slow	160	325
Moderate	180	350
Moderately hot	200	400
Hot	220	425
Very hot	240	475

Index

are media books

Published in 2024 by Are Media Books, Australia.
Are Media Books is a division of Are Media Pty Ltd.

ARE MEDIA
Chief Executive Officer Jane Huxley
General Manager Lifestyle & Food
Nicole Byers

NEW IDEA FOOD
Food Editor Karen Buckley
Content Director Alix Davis
Content Creator & Co-ordinator
Bec O'Reilly
Books Director David Scotto
Copy Editor Stephanie Kistner

Recipe Development Jane Ash, Karen Buckley, Mel Burge, Vikki Moursellas, Bec O'Reilly, Kerrie Worner
Photographers Ben Dearnley, Joe Filshie, Nic Gossage, Benito Martin, Andre Martin, James Moffatt, John Paul Urizar
Stylists Janelle Bloom, Carolyn Fienberg
Photochefs Sarah-Jane Hallett, Kim Meredith, Vikki Moursellas, Arum Shim, Amal Webster, Kerrie Worner

Printed in China by
Leo Paper Products.

A catalogue record for this book is available from the National Library of Australia.
ISBN 978-1-76122-185-9

Published by Are Media Books, a division of Are Media Pty Limited, 54 Park St, Sydney; GPO Box 4088, Sydney, NSW 2001, Australia
Ph +61 2 9282 8000;
www.aremediabooks.com.au

Order books
phone 1300 322 007 (within Australia) or order online at
www.aremediabooks.com.au